WRITTEN ENGLISH

Second edition with Practice Tests

DON SHIACH

Other titles in this series:

Basic Grammar	Don Shiach	ISBN	0 7195 7028 X
Basic Punctuation	Don Shiach	ISBN	0 7195 7027 1
Basic Spelling	Michael Temple	ISBN	0 7195 7026 3

Acknowledgements

The authors and publishers are grateful to the following for permission to include material in the text:

p.120 *An Equal Music* by Vikram Seth, Weidenfeld & Nicolson; p.121 *That's Not What I Meant!* by Deborah Tannen, J. M. Dent/Virago Press; p.123 *America Day by Day* by Simone De Beauvoir, Victor Gollancz; p.124 *A Better Class of Person* by John Osborne, Faber & Faber; pp.126–27 *The God of Small Things* by Arundhati Roy, HarperCollins Publishers Ltd; p.128 Part-time work, © *The Guardian*, Jobs and Money Section, 14 October 2000; p.130 *Man and Boy* by Tony Parsons, HarperCollins Publishers Ltd; p.131 *Starcarbon* by Ellen Gilchrist, Little, Brown and Company; pp.132–33 *Brighton Rock* by Graham Greene, Random House, reprinted by permission David Higham Associates; pp.134–35 *Yellowstone* by Hugh Crandall, © KC Publications 1997; p.137 *Journey from the North*, volume 1 by Storm Jameson, Virago.

Layouts by Rachel Griffin
Illustrations by Art Construction and David Farris
Typeset by Servis Filmsetting Ltd, Manchester
Printed and bound in Great Britain by the Alden Group, Oxford.

A CIP record for this book is available from the British Library.

ISBN 0 7195 7036 0

C24705

CONTENTS

Introduction 1
    What will this book do for me? 1
    How will this book help me? 2
    Putting it into practice 2
    Standard English and everyday language 3

Self-assessment questionnaire 4

PART A THE BASIC PRINCIPLES 11
1 Writing in sentences 12
    Simple sentences 15
    Compound sentences 17
    Complex sentences 21

2 Punctuation 28
    Punctuating sentences 28
    Capital letters 34
    Punctuating direct speech 36
    Colons and semi-colons 38
    The use of the apostrophe 40

3 Writing in paragraphs 43
    Setting out paragraphs 43
    What is a paragraph? 45
    Continuity 47

4 Spelling 50
    Spelling rules? 50
    Plurals 51
    Some common errors 52
    Spelling list 53
    A word about spellchecks 55

PART B ENGLISH AT WORK 59
Introduction 60
5 Communications: letters, memos, notes, faxes and e-mails 61
    Formal and informal writing 61
    More about letter writing 65
    Paragraphing letters 69
    Writing notes and memos 72
    Memos at work 74
    Sending faxes and e-mails 77

6   Note taking, summarising, report writing   80
       Skimming and scanning   80
       Highlighting and giving emphasis to text   81
       Taking notes and writing summaries   83
       Report writing   86

7   Agendas and minutes   89
       Drawing up an agenda   89
       Keeping minutes   91

8   Applying for jobs   94
       A general letter of enquiry   95
       Replying to job advertisements   97
       Writing a CV   99
       Filling in a job application form   102

Answers to Self-assessment questionnaire   106

Answers to Checkpoints and Activities   108

PART C PRACTICE TESTS   119
Introduction   119
Practice Test 1   120
Practice Test 2   126
Practice Test 3   132

INTRODUCTION

WHAT WILL THIS BOOK DO FOR ME?

This book is intended to enable you to improve the structure and presentation of your use of written language, so that you can express yourself clearly and make a good impression when it is important to do so. If the way you communicate is not clear, people may not make the effort to understand.

There are many occasions when it will be a great advantage if your written English is of a good standard – some will be part of education or training, while others crop up at work or in organising various aspects of your life.

The following table shows some of the more obvious examples of situations or tasks in which your grasp of written English will make a difference to how well you perform.

In education/ training	Organising everyday life	At work
Writing in a test or examination	Applying for a job	Writing letters to employees of other companies
Writing reports or essays	Writing to an organisation to make a request, enquiry or complaint	Placing orders or making enquiries
Summarising	Communicating with banks, solicitors, landlords etc.	Summarising
Note taking		Note taking
		Writing agendas or taking minutes for meetings
		Writing memos
		Writing faxes and e-mails

HOW WILL THIS BOOK HELP ME?

Part A of the book concentrates on the basic structures of written English and shows how using these structures correctly will make your writing clearer and more effective. In particular, it explains:

- how to construct **sentences** correctly and appropriately
- how to **punctuate** sentences
- how to structure your writing in **paragraphs**
- the key rules of **spelling**.

Part B of the book shows how each of these core writing skills is useful in several practical contexts, such as those listed in the table on page 1.

Part C of the book consists of three **Practice Tests** modelled on the English test papers that are taken at the end of Key Stage 3 in England and Wales.

If you are not sure where your strengths and weaknesses lie, the first thing you should do is to use the **Self-assessment questionnaire** on page 4 as a check of your own strengths and weaknesses. You can then concentrate on those areas where you need most practice.

PUTTING IT INTO PRACTICE

Making the transfer between acquiring knowledge and putting it into practice is the crucial test for any new skill. Learning conventions and rules is pointless unless you are able to apply them. In this book, you will be given plenty of opportunities in the **Checkpoints** and **Activities** to use the structures and skills you have learnt and to check that you are using them appropriately by consulting the answers given on pages 106–117.

STANDARD ENGLISH AND EVERYDAY LANGUAGE

Standard English means the type of English that is conventionally used in education, in business, in the media and most written communications, and in most other contexts that are 'public' rather than 'private'. You also need a knowledge of the grammar of Standard English for situations when you need to communicate clearly with people whose everyday English may not be the same as yours.

Standard English is generally more formal than the type of English we are accustomed to using in communicating with our friends, family and local community. Most of us, for example, are familiar with a dialect of English which has, to a certain extent, its own separate vocabulary and set of grammatical rules. It is not true that Standard English has grammar and our own everyday English does not; remember that grammar **describes** every use of language. It is also not the case that Standard English has to sound pompous and fussy. It is meant to be an aid to clear communication, not an obstacle.

Consider these examples:

We was only playing a friendly.

I'm no going there tonight.

Consider – Kaf karid
tixgalin – ku xisaabtamid

Both these statements might be quite appropriate in the context of an informal situation among people familiar with these 'dialect' features (remember, a dialect is a version of a language shared by some, but not all, speakers of that language). However, they would be considered 'incorrect' in terms of Standard English.

When you want to create a favourable impression, and leave no room for doubt as to what you mean, applying the rules of Standard English enables you to reach a wider audience than if you use a grammar that might be appropriate in much more informal situations, such as when you are with family and friends.

dialect – lahjad

extent – fidsanay Certain – hubaal – gar garkeed

waasac ahaan
heer – xad

SELF-ASSESSMENT QUESTIONNAIRE

To test your present level of skill in basic written English, try the following questionnaire. Then check the answers and see what your results tell you about your strengths and weaknesses, and which sections of this book will help to raise the level of your skills. Award yourself one mark for each correct answer, but subtract one mark for each incorrect answer (changing something that was originally correct).

WRITING IN SENTENCES

1 Read the following article. Several errors have been made in the punctuation of sentences. Pick these out and rewrite the report inserting the correct punctuation.

the level of pollution on British beaches is decreasing This is according to a report produced by an environmental group who investigated the state of beaches up and down the country what is a satisfactory level of pollution, however Stating that most British beaches have improved is not saying very much, the previous situation was downright scandalous with horror stories of sewage and chemical pollution, the truth is there should be no pollution on any of our beaches. with more and more British people taking British summer holidays rather than European package tours, it is more than ever important that beaches are clean and healthy places for our kids

(11 marks)

2 Read the following letter. The writer intended to write in complete sentences, but has included several incomplete sentences. Pick out these incomplete sentences.

Dear Sir,

I regret to have to return to you the enclosed item. Not a good buy because it broke when it was first used. I am an old customer of your firm and am surprised that this has occurred. Always been satisfied in the past.

Asking for a refund rather than a replacement. Because I have no confidence in the product now. This does not mean I will not order from your catalogue in the future. As I do appreciate the convenience of ordering goods by post. Since I am old and cannot get to shops.

Looking forward to receiving the refund.

Yours faithfully,

E. Braithwaite

E. Braithwaite

regret —ucacan pca xumahay shalaayto gonaaneyn

(7 marks)

3 Pick out the **main** or **principal** clause in each of the following sentences.

a) Although I am by nature a happy person, lately I have been feeling very down, because several sad events have occurred in my life.

b) The woman bought the most expensive handbag in the shop, which pleased the salesman immensely because he was working on commission.

c) When I rang your number last night, I got the engaged signal, which continued for the next hour or so.

d) As the government had such a small majority and was very unpopular in the country, the by-election was being dreaded because it would further increase its difficulties.

e) Do not return until I say that you can.

f) Forget that I said that.

g) The man, who was a complete stranger to all of them, appeared very friendly.

h) Because I was late, the teacher was angry with me, which did not improve my chances of getting a good report, although I felt that I deserved a second chance.

i) The tournament had been a great success, because the crowds had been huge, which had pleased the sponsors, who had invested a large amount of money.

(9 marks) **5**

Assess what you know about writing in sentences by checking your answers with those on page 106.

Award one mark for each correct answer and subtract one mark for each incorrect answer. Then check your total marks against the advice given below.

Score more than 23 out of 27: your knowledge of writing in sentences is good.

Score between 19 and 22: you need to look carefully at Chapter 1.

Score less than 19: your knowledge of writing in sentences is limited; work your way through Chapter 1.

PUNCTUATION

1 Read the following memorandum. It consists of a number of sentences, but it lacks capital letters and full stops. Decide where one sentence ends and another begins and insert capital letters and full stops appropriately.

it has been decided that an extra weekly practice night will take place during this month the committee believes that, with such important games coming up, this additional commitment will be very important fielding practice will take priority this has let the team down in recent matches every member of the first team squad is expected to turn up if there is any difficulty about this, the individual concerned must discuss the reasons with the team captain this decision was unanimous we want success in the league and the cup this season surely we all believe that such success is within our grasp the committee confidently expects the support of every player in this extra endeavour let's look forward to winning some trophies

Commitment = balangaad

(22 marks)

2 Read the following newspaper report. Capital letters have been used at the beginning of sentences but they have been left out in numerous other instances when they are needed. Rewrite the report, inserting capital letters where they are appropriate.

bopper, the very successful independent record company, has just announced it has signed the new sensation of the pop world, the pepper pots, to a recording contract. A spokesperson for the company, roger maynard, said yesterday that sales of the group's discs had soared in several countries, including america, britain, australia, japan and germany. gayle russell, the lead singer, said she was delighted with the deal and it was especially good news on the eve of the start of the group's world tour. 'We're off to europe tomorrow and then we take in africa, asia and south america. It's a long way from bermondsey,' she added with a grin. The 'new musical express' reported that the group's income over the last year exceeded ten million pounds, while 'hello' magazine is reported to have offered a huge sum for exclusive pictures of the world tour. Only 'the guardian' and 'the times' struck a sour note: most of their readers, they reported, have never heard of the pots. 'They don't like us, we don't care,' retorted jimmy lou harris, another member of the group.

(30 marks)

3 Read the following extract from a story. Direct speech has been used, but it has not been punctuated. Rewrite the passage inserting punctuation where you think it is appropriate.

Judy assumed her most sarcastic tone.

you're not trying to tell me most designer fashion is meant to be worn she said most of it is just ridiculous.

people wear it all the time Melanie responded they pay a lot of money for those clothes

more fool them said Judy

I wish I could afford one of those designer dresses insisted Melanie I will one day

you must be crazy said Judy you'd look silly in them

you said Melanie are just jealous

jealous exclaimed Judy who's jealous why would I be jealous now tell me that

because you know replied Melanie that you wouldn't look good in really fashionable clothes

what a load of baloney exclaimed Judy just who do you think you are

(76 marks)

4 In the following notes, apostrophes have sometimes been incorrectly used. In some instances, they have, however, been correctly inserted. Rewrite each of the notes, correcting the use of the apostrophe where you think it is needed.

a)

Its on for this evening! The restaurants booked, the cars gearbox has been fixed and alls' well with the world. Ill be home by five at the latest. My good suits at the cleaners. Itd be great if youd pick it up for me. The cats food is in the cupboard. Its going to be a great evening out. Im really looking forward to it.   Jim

(10 marks)

b)

This memos all Id time to leave you. Its all go this end. The deals on. I cant see therell be any problem's. The moneys settled and the date's have been agreed. I'll give you a detailed outline once the contracts with us. Congratulation's all round are due. Weve put a lot of effort into this. Its really great to have landed the work.   Jenny.

(13 marks)

Assess what you know about punctuation by checking your answers with those on pages 106 and 107.

Award one mark for each correct answer and subtract one mark for each incorrect answer. Then check your total marks against the advice given below.

Score more than 135 out of 151: your knowledge of punctuation is good.

Score between 95 and 134: you need to look carefully at Chapter 2.

Score less than 95: your knowledge of punctuation is limited; work your way through Chapter 2.

WRITING IN PARAGRAPHS

The following letter is a general letter of enquiry about employment. It has been written without using paragraphs. Rewrite the letter dividing it into appropriate paragraphs.

Dear Sir/Madam

I am writing to enquire about the possibility of being employed in your firm as a junior office clerk. I am sixteen years of age, have just left school and have several passes at GCSE level. These include Business Studies, English, Maths, French and Statistics. I have attended Boxley High School for the last six years. While at school, I took part in a Job Experience scheme during which I worked in a solicitor's office. I found this work experience very interesting and rewarding. It gave me invaluable experience of office life. I can also supply relevant references from the school and the solicitor's office where I was on Job Experience. I am very keen to join your firm and feel confident I can fulfil any duties that would be handed to me. I am available for interview at any time. I look forward to hearing from you in the near future.

Yours faithfully

Michelle Nichols

Michelle Nichols

(6 marks)

Assess what you know about writing in paragraphs by checking your answers with those on page 107.

Award one mark for each correct answer and subtract one mark for each incorrect answer. Then check your total marks against the advice given below.

Score 5 or 6: you know about writing in paragraphs.
Score 3 or 4: you need to look carefully at Chapter 3.
Score less than 3: your knowledge of writing in paragraphs is limited; work your way through Chapter 3.

SPELLING

Read the following newspaper report. It contains numerous spelling errors. Pick these out and rewrite the report with the correct spellings.

Maneger in Despute with Refferee

Jocky Malone, the manger of Baykop United, was involvd in a vilent argement with referie Joe Reid during Satrday's match at Friar Rode.

After a United gaol was disalowed, Malone, nown as 'Jaws' in footbal circels, was scene to gestikulate at Reid and mak menecing mouves towrds him. Malone had to be restraned by his coleages.

'I was'nt awar of the insident at the tyme,' said the ref, 'but if I had bean, I wuld have ordred Mr Malone from the touch-lin.'

'Jaws' Malone has alredy bean worned on sevral ocasions, the last tim for head-buting another maneger. The Fotball Leage ar likly to take a very glomy veiw of this latest incdent in the picturesc carer of this contreversal persenlity.

'I denie shouteing obsenites at the ref,' said an unrepentent Malone after the mach. 'I was only leting of steem. Surly I shuld be givn the fredom to do that. Im not a crimnal after all.'

(64 marks)

Assess what you know about spelling by checking your answers with those on page 107.

   Award one mark for each correct answer and subtract one mark for each incorrect answer. Then check your total marks against the advice given below.

   Score more than 60 out of 64: your spelling ability is good.
   Score between 48 and 59: you need to look carefully at Chapter 4.
   Score less than 48: your spelling ability is limited; work your way through Chapter 4.

PART A
THE BASIC PRINCIPLES

1

WRITING IN
SENTENCES

In speech, you will use many incomplete sentences. When you are putting down in written form the actual words that people have said, you will also use incomplete sentences.

However, in more formal writing, you should use very few, if any, incomplete sentences. One of the keys to competent writing in English is to be able to use complete and grammatically correct sentences.

Sentences **make a statement**:

The best things in life are free.

Or they **give an instruction**:

```
KEEP OFF THE GRASS.
```

Or they **ask a question**:

May I help you?

The essential thing to remember about **complete sentences** is that they make sense on their own. **Incomplete sentences** may make sense, but only within a surrounding context of other sentences or phrases. For example, this is an incomplete sentence:

'Yes.'

On its own, it has no real meaning. However, it acquires meaning if it is seen in its **context**:

'Do you like frozen yoghurt?'
'Yes.'

The incomplete sentence 'Yes.' is the abbreviated version of the complete sentence 'Yes, I like frozen yoghurt.' In speech, there is no need to repeat the part about liking frozen yoghurt in response to the question. The 'Yes' makes it clear what the speaker means.

However, when you are writing, it is important to use complete sentences. Look at this extract from a job application form, in which the applicant has been asked to write about herself. Read it aloud to yourself.

> I think I am qualified for the post. Because I gained good grades in the relevant GCSE examinations. I also like children a lot. And work well with people of my own age. Perhaps because I have younger and older brothers and sisters in my family.

When you read the passage aloud, you probably noticed something awkward about it. It didn't seem to 'hang together' properly. That was because the writer used three incomplete sentences, which did not make sense on their own. These incomplete sentences are not acceptable in formal writing such as this.

Here is the corrected version, with complete sentences. Read it aloud, noting how each of the sentences now makes sense on its own.

> I think I am qualified for the post, because I gained good grades in the relevant GCSE examinations. I also like children a lot and work well with people of my own age, perhaps because I have younger and older brothers and sisters in my family.

The incomplete sentences have disappeared. They have been joined up to complete sentences to make longer, **complex** sentences.

In your writing, you must aim to write in complete sentences that make sense and are correctly constructed.

Another key to writing in correctly constructed sentences lies in the punctuation of sentences.

Sentences must start with a capital letter and end with a full stop, question mark or an exclamation mark.

1 Britain must commit itself to Europe.

2 Where do we go from here?

3 This is a total farce!

Sentence 1 is in the form of a statement. It requires a full stop at the end.

Sentence 2 is in the form of a question, so it requires a question mark.

Sentence 3 is an exclamation, so it needs an exclamation mark. (For a more detailed explanation of the punctuation of sentences, see Section 1 in *Basic Punctuation*, a companion book in this series.)

There are three types of basic sentences: **simple**, **compound** and **complex**.

In your writing, there will be opportunities to use all three kinds.

Sometimes it is appropriate to use shorter sentences in the form of simple sentences. At other times, it will be appropriate to use longer sentences in the form of compound, complex and multiple sentences (see page 17).

13

✓ Checkpoint A

Read aloud the following letter that someone has written to a bank manager. Identify where incomplete sentences have been used.

Dear Sir

In answer to your letter about my account being overdrawn. I would like to point out that my account has never been overdrawn before. An unfortunate oversight on my part.

To avoid this situation arising again, I would like to arrange for a permanent overdraft facility. Once again apologies. Not intentional on my part. I will ensure, in future, that I have enough money in my account to cover any cheques that I write.

Looking forward to receiving an application form.

Yours faithfully

J. P. Morgan

J. P. Morgan

Activities 1 and 2

1 Rewrite the above letter, using only complete sentences that make sense on their own.

2 Read the following job description. Once again, incomplete sentences have been used. Rewrite the passage, using only complete sentences.

The duties of the assistant storesperson include the logging of entries in the relevant stock book. Storing in the appropriate section. In addition, making a record of when staff request particular equipment. The storesperson must also receive orders of supplies as they arrive from the central stores. A strict record of all such supplies must be kept. To stand in for the senior storesperson when she or he is absent. Facilitating the supply of equipment. The assistant storesperson has the authority, in the absence of the senior storeperson, to sign out equipment to authorised personnel.

SIMPLE SENTENCES

The following are examples of simple sentences:

1 Shall we see that film?
2 I'm going to Majorca for my holidays.
3 Give it to me straight.
4 Hey, that's not fair!

Sentence 1 asks a question and has one verb 'shall see'.

Sentence 2 makes a statement and has one verb 'am going' (shortened to 'm going').

Sentence 3 gives an instruction and has one verb 'give'.

Sentence 4 makes an exclamation (an expression of surprise) and has one verb 'is' (shortened to 's).

A simple sentence makes complete sense on its own, but it need not be short:

Despite the gloomy forecast, and to their complete delight, the day of the picnic, chosen at random by Aunt Mabel, turned out to be gloriously sunny, especially high on the Downs, the site of the feast.

In spite of its length, this remains a simple sentence because it makes one statement and has one main verb, 'turned'. Here is another example of another long simple sentence:

Lacking an effective fast bowler, the county, defending a small total after the collapse of their batting, were forced to rely on spinners, much to the delight of their opponents' leading batsmen.

This simple sentence makes complete sense on its own; it makes one statement and has only one finite verb 'were forced'. (A finite verb has a subject.)

So, although simple sentences need not be all that brief, one of the advantages of using them is to make a point concisely and economically:

Violence on the football pitch must be stamped out.

The latest trade figures show a decline in activity.

The battle of Waterloo ended Napoleon's hopes of dominating Europe.

Each of these sentences makes one point simply and directly. There will be many occasions in your own writing when you will want to do that.

■ BASIC TYPES OF SIMPLE SENTENCES

Simple sentences have four basic structures:

• Type 1: a subject plus the verb 'to be'
All the following sentences are of this type:

Brown bread is healthier than white.

The weather forecast could have been more accurate.

There are no easy solutions.

What were your guiding principles in drawing up this plan?

In these simple sentences, the subject(s) – the person(s) or thing(s) which the sentence is about – **'is'**, **'could have been'**, **'are'** or **'were'** something.

• **Type 2: a subject does something**
There may be an adverb or adverbial phrase attached to the verb.

The dog <u>growled</u>.
            verb

I <u>ran</u> <u>quickly</u> down the street.
 verb *adverb*

The police <u>came</u>   <u>out of the van</u>.
             verb *adverbial phrase*

The spectators <u>groaned</u>   <u>in unison</u>.
                 verb   *adverbial phrase*

In this type of simple sentence, there is someone or something that performs the action and there is the action itself.

• **Type 3: a subject does something to someone or something**
All the the verbs in this type of simple sentence have an **object**.

  <u>He</u>   <u>challenged</u> his <u>rival</u> to a duel.
Subject   *verb*   *object*

  <u>She</u>   <u>was writing</u> a <u>novel</u>.
Subject   *verb*   *object*

<u>Forget</u> all your <u>troubles</u>.
 verb   *object*

  <u>He</u>   <u>is building</u> a <u>house</u> to his own design.
Subject   *verb*   *object*

• **Type 4: a subject appears to be, seems, becomes, feels or looks**
The outcome appears to be a foregone conclusion.

There seemed to be no possible solution to the crisis.

The couple became more and more angry.

The patient felt satisfied with her hospital treatment.

Prospects looked rosy for the organisation.

(For a more detailed analysis of these types of simple sentences, consult the *More about Sentences* section of *Basic Grammar*, another book in this series.)

3 Complete the following appropriately, using the type of simple sentence indicated: 1, 2, 3 or 4.

   a) The police ....(type 1)

   b) From the deep cave emerged.................................(type 2)

   c) The circus clown...(type 3)

   d) The politicians ....(type 4)

   e) Interestingly, most pupils......................................(type 1)

   f) The supporters..(type 2)

   g) For the last time, the star......................................(type 3)

   h) In spite of everything, the holiday-makers ....(type 4)

4 Add to the following simple sentences any words or phrases to elaborate on the topic. Keep them simple, so that each sentence still has only one verb and makes only one statement.

   a) The birds gathered.

   b) The crowd were shattered.

   c) The situation became worse.

   d) The newsreader introduced the report.

   e) She appeared normal.

   f) The audience laughed.

   g) Justice was done.

   h) The man felt worse.

   i) The hunter fired the gun.

COMPOUND SENTENCES

Compound sentences (sometimes called **double sentences**) are basically two simple sentences joined by **'and'**, **'but'** or **'or'**.

1 Shall we dance or shall we sit this one out?

2 The government increased taxes and reduced benefits.

3 Give me my fair share, but keep enough for yourself.

4 The clown fell off the horse and the audience roared with laughter.

Sentence 1 combines two simple sentences (in the form of questions) joined by **'or'**. Note the two verbs, **'shall dance'** and **'shall sit'**, one in each part of the sentence.

Sentence 2 combines two simple sentences joined by **'and'**. Note the two verbs, **'increased'** and **'reduced'**, one in each part. However, both parts share the same subject **'government'**, which does not need to be repeated.

Sentence 3 combines two simple sentences (in the form of instructions), joined by '**but**'. Note the two verbs, '**give**' and '**keep**', one in each part. The subject 'you' is understood.

Sentence 4 combines two simple sentences joined by '**and**'. Note the two verbs, '**fell**' and '**roared**', one in each part. In this example (unlike sentence 2), the two parts have different subjects.

■ 'AND', 'BUT' AND 'OR'

'And', 'but' and 'or' are the main joining words or **conjunctions** used in compound sentences.

ANTONY CONJUNCTION
AND
HELENA RELATIVE-PRONOUN

IN

THE COMPLEX SENTENCE

A JOINING WORDS
PRODUCTION

'And' joins two sentences that have a close link, although each part of the compound sentence may have a different subject:

Jesse James was shot in the back by Bob Howard and Frank James disappeared into obscurity.

England face a tough task in their group and Scotland will meet some of the toughest teams in the tournament in theirs.

Job opportunities are beginning to increase and the unemployment figures are expected to fall.

'But' joins two sentences that express a contrast:

> I like mainly French food, but she prefers British cuisine.
> Our party stands for freedom, but our opponents preach state control.
> Mark likes most kinds of music, but hates rock-and-roll.

'Or' expresses an alternative.

> You may travel overnight or stay in a hotel.
> Customers may settle their accounts by cheque or use a credit card.
> Manchester United may capture the striker or Blackburn may beat them to it.

■ 'EITHER/OR' AND 'NEITHER/NOR'

These joining words or conjunctions may also be used as joining words in compound sentences.

> Either get down to some real work or leave our employment.
> Either Norman drives or Eileen can.

A longer version of a **compound sentence** is the **multiple sentence**. Multiple sentences consist of three or more simple sentences joined by **'and'**, **'or'** or **'but'**.

1 We can go this weekend or we can postpone it, but we have to go sometime.
2 This service provides guaranteed delivery and is recommended for items of small value, but more valuable items should be sent by registered air mail or you can choose to use surface mail.

Sentence 1 has three simple sentences joined by **'or'** and **'but'**.

Sentence 2 consists of four simple sentences: the first two are joined by **'and'** and share the same subject **'This service'**; the other two are connected by **'but'** and then **'or'**.

Here are some further examples of multiple sentences:

> Fish is a provider of protein and so is white meat, but too much red meat in your diet can be harmful.

> You may choose to travel by coach or opt for rail, but the quickest journey is by air and the most comfortable means is by ocean liner.

> Unfortunately, television is the favourite pastime of most people, but playing sport is also hugely popular. Reading has declined, or, at least, it appears to have done so, but these trends may alter.

Both compound and multiple sentences are useful in varying the length of your sentences and avoiding a 'bitty' and disjointed style in your writing. Take the opportunity in your writing to use a variety of sentences. However, you should be careful to avoid using too many compound sentences that are joined by 'and', as in this example:

> I would like to be a policewoman and I hope to be accepted soon as a trainee. I am looking forward to the training and I expect it to be challenging. I consider myself quite tough and resourceful and I am confident about making the grade. I have the necessary qualifications for the job and will do well in an interview. I am looking forward to starting in this career and I want to help people.

This is rather tedious and repetitive. Not only are there five sentences in succession that use '**and**' as the joining word, but each sentence follows exactly the same structure, each sentence within each compound sentence beginning with 'I'. More variety is required:

> I would like to be a policewoman and I hope to be accepted soon as a trainee. Happily, I am looking forward to the training, but I expect it to be challenging. I consider myself quite tough and resourceful and am confident about making the grade. Fortunately, I have the necessary qualifications for the job. I will also do well in an interview. As I want to help people, I am looking forward to starting in this career.

The second sentence of the new version starts with an adverb '**happily**' which helps to vary the structure. The joining word is '**but**' rather than '**and**'. The fourth sentence again uses the device of starting with an adverb and one of the original compound sentences is split into two simple sentences. The last sentence is now a complex sentence (see page 21), but the word order has been changed to avoid starting with 'I' again.

The new version is less repetitive and more varied.

Activities 5, 6 and 7

5 Change each of the examples below into either a compound or a multiple sentence, as appropriate.

   a) The referee blew the final whistle. The fans erupted with joy.

   b) The prosecutor made a convincing case. It was based on purely circumstantial evidence. The jury found the defendant not guilty.

   c) The management offered the employees a lump sum payment. The management advised acceptance.

   d) You may have your holidays in June. You can wait till August.

   e) The train was very late in arriving. The guard explained the circumstances. The passengers generally accepted the apology.

6 Read the following notice about a staff outing. It is written in a succession of simple sentences, which makes it repetitive and disjointed. Rewrite the notice using a combination of compound and multiple sentences.

The annual History Group outing will take place on July 27th. It will be to Southend. Those wishing to book a place will have to do so by July 15th. You may do this through your group leader. You may also inform Mr Greene. The total cost will be £18. This will include the cost of the hire of the coach. The cost of lunch and afternoon tea is also included. The coach will leave from outside the building at 9.00 a.m. It will return at 6.00 p.m. The History Group urge you to support the outing. We need to know numbers as soon as possible.

7 The following extract from a horoscope newspaper column uses only simple sentences. Rewrite it with the aim of making it less repetitive, using a combination of compound, multiple and complex sentences.

 Libra It is a good week for school work. Pocket money problems loom. Visitors could cause problems. You will feel happy. Now may be the time to start new interests. You may make some new friends.

 Sagittarius Take care to keep up to date with things. It could be a good time to plan your holiday. Avoid possible arguments with friends. Show resolve. School matters dominate.

 Scorpio You may face a challenge this week. It is time for imagination and initiative. Past good deeds on your part may pay off. At school, success may beckon. The opportunity to change courses may present itself.

 Capricorn Are you working too hard? A helping hand may be available. You should be full of creative ideas. Start planning for next year. It is time to mend some past disputes.

COMPLEX SENTENCES

Complex sentences consist of one **main clause** (a simple sentence that could stand on its own) and one or more **subordinate clauses** which are attached to this main clause. The main clause in each of these examples is underlined:

1 When the weather improves, <u>we will take a long holiday</u>.

This sentence consists of two clauses: the main clause, which is underlined, and one subordinate clause.

2 <u>The government decided</u> that it would raise interest rates because the economy was getting out of control.

This sentence has three clauses: the main clause (underlined) at the beginning of the sentence, and two other, subordinate clauses.

3 As soon as it is possible, <u>I will do</u> what I promised, although it will cause me great expense.

This sentence consists of four clauses: the main clause (underlined), a subordinate clause at the beginning of the sentence and two other subordinate clauses after the main one.

Note that each of the main clauses in these sentences makes sense on its own:

we will take a long holiday

the government decided

I will do what I promised

These 'simple sentences' are the core of the longer, complex sentences, which have been built round them.

Remember that a clause – even a subordinate one – must have a subject and a verb of its own. For example, in the subordinate clause 'when the weather improves', the subject is '**weather**' and the verb is '**improves**'.

The rest of the sentence is always built round the main clause. All the other parts of the sentence are **subordinate** or **dependent** on it. It might help to think of this main clause as a simple sentence within a complex one.

■ USING COMPLEX SENTENCES

Writing complex sentences allows you to develop a point or to give additional information within a single sentence.

To construct complex sentences correctly, there are two main groups of words that you will have to use: **conjunctions** or **joining words**, and **relative pronouns**.

* Conjunctions or joining words include these:

  when   where   how   if   until   because   as   in order that   so that
  that   what   whether   although   before   as long as   whereas
  despite the fact that   unless   whenever

* The relative pronouns are:

  who   whom   which   whose   that

You will need to use some of these words when you write complex sentences.

Here are some more examples of complex sentences which use **conjunctions** to join the main clause to the other parts or clauses in the sentence. The main clause in each sentence is underlined, as are the joining words.

Unless the bill is paid within ten days, the board will have to cut supplies, although this is a matter of great regret to the company.

Before they arrived at the resort, they had planned exactly what they wanted to do, because they had such a short time at their disposal.

Whereas she liked the theatre and ballet, he preferred the cinema and reading, but this did not cause problems, because both were tolerant of the other's tastes.

Notice that one of the conjunctions used in the last sentence is 'but', which is usually used to join the two parts of a compound or double sentence. This last example of a complex sentence is also, in part, a compound sentence because it has two main clauses in it.

Look at these examples of complex sentences in which **relative pronouns** have been used as the connecting words between the main clause and the other parts of the sentences.

They bought the house whose owner lived abroad.

The woman who discovered the body was only a visitor to the town, which was thoroughly shocked by the murder.

The economic benefits that we all hope for will come in the near future, which will inspire confidence in future investment.

The principal whom you all admire is about to retire, which represents a great loss to the college that she has led for so many years.

Now look at these complex sentences in which a mixture of conjunctions and relative pronouns have been used.

Although France fought hard to equalise, Germany held out till the final whistle, which came as a great relief to their hard-pressed defence.

Until I hear from you, I will take no action, because I must have your authority to act, which is quite usual in these situations, unless the circumstances are extraordinary, which might lead to a special dispensation being made.

Whoever takes the lead, that person must be decisive, because we cannot afford to delay any longer, which must be clear to anyone who has analysed our situation in detail.

In your own writing, there will be opportunities for you to write longer, complex sentences. Indeed, it is a sign of a mature style to be able to do so. However, you must feel confident about handling the structure of such sentences. They must 'hang together' logically and grammatically.

Complex sentences are appropriate in your own writing when you want to express something more complicated than can be expressed in a simple or compound sentence. Complex sentences allow you to include additional or descriptive information. Often you will use complex sentences when you are arguing a case or giving an explanation that requires detail or qualification.

✓ Checkpoint B

1 Decide whether each of the following is a simple, multiple or complex sentence.

a) Do you know whether the last train has left?

b) You may use double cream or, if you are worried about gaining weight, you can substitute fromage frais.

c) The team was playing badly and the players were lacking fight, but the manager refused to alter his tactics.

d) This town isn't big enough for both of us.

e) After the rain had stopped, a beautiful rainbow appeared in the sky, which cheered everybody up.

f) Employees may wish to take ten days' holiday over the Christmas and New Year period, or they may choose to take a shorter break and add the extra days to their summer holiday.

2 Pick out the main clause (the 'simple sentence') that is at the heart of each of the following complex sentences and around which each of the sentences is built.

a) Although the sun was shining, the temperature never climbed above 60°C, because there was a chilling breeze from the east.

b) The garden began to bloom in April, so that they were forced to mow the lawn, which did not please them at all.

c) When I am reading a book that I enjoy, I am lost in a world of my own because I become completely absorbed in the story.

d) Because you are now a mature person and able to make up your own mind about issues, although at times you do not act that way, the trustees feel that you can be trusted to make decisions on your own.

e) If you purchase one sofa and the sale is completed before September 30th, you are eligible to buy another exactly the same at a reduced price, which is a real bonus.

Activities 8–14

8 Build a complex sentence from each of the following simple sentences. The number of subordinate clauses you should add is shown in brackets.

a) The parents hurriedly packed their cases. (2)

b) The film was not popular in Britain. (3)

c) The police siren echoed across the city. (1)

d) The workmen toiled over the extension all day. (4)

e) The bidding became very fierce at the auction. (2)

9 Transform each of the simple sentences below into a complex sentence by adding one or more clauses, using *conjunctions* as the connecting words.

   a) The train arrived late at its destination.
   b) You can forget that.
   c) She was that type of person.
   d) In spring, the garden must be renewed.
   e) Crime statistics are notoriously misleading.
   f) Failure to comply is a serious offence.
   g) Applicants must be experienced.
   h) I can offer many relevant qualifications.

10 Transform each of the simple sentences below into a complex sentence by adding one or more clauses, using only *relative pronouns* as the connecting words.

   a) The woman gave a very impressive speech.
   b) The hero of the film was incredibly brave.
   c) Laughter is a great healer.
   d) Many contributions were made.
   e) We are witnessing the end of an era.
   f) Computer technology has made great advances.
   g) Proceed to the loading bay.
   h) Can you give me an answer?

11 Below are some more simple sentences. This time, add clauses to make them into complex sentences, but use a combination of conjunctions (including '**and**', '**or**' and '**but**') and relative pronouns as connecting words.

   a) Mention that to him.
   b) The legal consequences are far-reaching.
   c) The priest said the prayer.
   d) Perhaps there is room for doubt after all.
   e) The appointment will be made in two weeks' time.
   f) You must always issue a receipt to customers.
   g) Every option was considered.
   h) Into every life a little rain must fall.

12 The following notice uses only simple sentences. This makes it read awkwardly. It would be better if some of these sentences were joined together to form compound sentences. Rewrite the notice accordingly.

> **Each employee must attend one residential course per year. There will be a selection to choose from. It is obligatory to choose at least one. The management consider this an essential part of every employee's training. Special circumstances, for example, family obligations, will be taken into account. Advice is available from the training department. You may also consult your supervisor. There will be no cost to employees for the course. All travelling expenses will be refunded.**

13 Read the following article. It consists of a succession of simple sentences. Rewrite it using conjunctions to form complex and compound sentences.

The world of work can be daunting for many school-leavers. Instead of a cosy school or college environment, young people are often faced with a large anonymous organisation. This organisation may appear not to care much for the individual. The new, young employee may feel lost. Some firms are aware of the problem. They look after new employees. Others dismally fail to do so.

In a situation like this, it is easy for young people to feel alienated. They may develop anti-work attitudes. Low morale may result.

An attitude of doing as little as possible may take hold. This is not good for the young person. It is not productive for the employer.

Firms must have a reception policy for new employees. They must appoint experienced and sympathetic members of staff to take care of young people in particular. This policy will pay off in the future. Firms should want their staff to stay with them. Staff loyalty has to be earned. A happy employee is a productive employee. Each member of the work-force should feel part of the organisation.

14 The following letter uses nothing but simple sentences. The result is a disjointed style that makes it difficult to read. Rewrite the letter, expanding simple sentences into complex or compound sentences where you think this is appropriate.

Dear Sir/Madam

I am writing to complain. It is about a pair of trousers. I bought them from your mail order firm last month.

I wore the trousers on only a few occasions. I found that they were coming apart in several places. The only explanation was the poor quality of the material. They certainly were not damaged by me. I am very disappointed with the quality of the goods. The trousers were not like those shown in your catalogue.

I am returning the trousers in a separate package. In the circumstances, I am asking for a complete refund. This is only fair. I will not accept a credit note. I would like a speedy response to this letter.

I look forward to hearing from you.

Yours faithfully

Lorna Jones

SKILLCHECK Check these statements to assess what you have learnt from this chapter. If you cannot honestly tick all of these statements, then go back over the relevant section.

❏ I can recognise the various types of sentences: simple, compound and complex.

❏ I understand how to use conjunctions and relative pronouns in writing complex sentences.

❏ I appreciate that a variety of sentence structure in any extended piece of writing avoids monotony of style.

2

PUNCTUATION

■ **Punctuation helps you to communicate clearly in written English.**

■ **Without punctuation, any piece of writing becomes much harder to understand:**

> **Drivers can take certain precautions to avoid having an accident never speed even when you are late for an appointment do not take chances in overtaking situations be alert to danger signs and read the road ahead never drink and drive take frequent rests when on a long journey maintain your car in a roadworthy condition check tyre pressures and oil levels**

■ **This can be understood, but the lack of punctuation makes it much harder. With appropriate punctuation, the task becomes much easier:**

> **Drivers can take certain precautions to avoid having an accident. Never speed, even when you are late for an appointment. Do not take chances in overtaking situations. Be alert to danger signs and read the road ahead. Never drink and drive. Take frequent rests when on a long journey. Maintain your car in a roadworthy condition. Check tyre pressures and oil levels.**

PUNCTUATING SENTENCES

In the previous chapter, you read that all sentences start with a capital letter and end with a full stop.

Knowing where one sentence ends and another begins is an essential skill in applying punctuation rules.

If you are in any doubt about that, read what you have written aloud or 'in your head'. The flow of meaning should tell you where you should put a full stop (or a question mark or exclamation mark, if appropriate). Start the next sentence with a capital letter.

The punctuation of simple sentences is straightforward: start with a capital letter and end with a full stop. However, within a simple sentence, you may also have to insert one or more commas:

For example, you could choose art as an option.

Here a comma is required after the interjection **'for example'**.

If the sentence had a slightly different word order, then a pair of commas would be required:

You could, for example, choose art as an option.

Here is a list of common interjections requiring commas in this way:

for example   however   nevertheless   of course   on the other hand
perhaps   similarly   yet   without doubt   well   mind you

Then there are the more 'emotional' and colloquial interjections that express surprise, joy, anger and various other feelings:

<u>Ah</u>, now I understand . . .   <u>Ouch</u>, that hurt!   <u>Hear, hear</u>, I couldn't agree more.

Interjections require single or double commas depending on where they come in the sentence:

However, an alternative would be drama.
An alternative, however, would be drama.

Of course, science would be another option.
Science, of course, would be another option.

Mind you, that would be the last straw.
That, mind you, would be the last straw.

A useful variation when you are writing simple sentences is to use an adverb as the first word, as in the following examples. If you do this, a comma is required after the adverb.

Surprisingly, chemistry is not offered as an option.
Angrily, the representative refused the offer.

The same rule applies to compound sentences. Generally, if the two parts of a compound sentence are joined by **'but'**, then a comma is required:

It should produce results, but there is no way of knowing for sure.

If interjections are added, it is usual to use commas to punctuate:

It should, of course, produce results, but there is no way of knowing for sure.

Similarly, if an adverb is added, it needs to be surrounded by commas.

It should, of course, produce results, but, unfortunately, there is no way of knowing for sure.

Another pair of commas is required when an 'explanation' is inserted in the sentence, as in these examples:

> The teacher, Mr Reid, was considered to be very strict.
>
> Freud's most famous theory, the Oedipus Complex, has been denounced as nonsense by many experts.
>
> The Tower, Blackpool's most famous landmark, is a must for all visitors.

In complex sentences it is usual to separate clauses with commas:

> When the last lap started, the British runner was four metres behind,
>   *subordinate clause*   *main clause*
> which presented her with a formidable task.
>   *subordinate clause*

Here is another example of the punctuation of a different structure in a complex sentence:

> The weekly programme about rock music, which was transmitted after eleven o'clock, was very controversial, principally because the young presenters used street language most of the time, which infuriated some viewers, although it appealed to much of its huge audience.

The use of commas to punctuate complex sentences in this way makes it easier for your readers to understand what you are saying.

A variation in the use of commas in punctuating complex sentences occurs according to what you are trying to communicate. Look at these very similar sentences:

1 The players, who had done their very best to win the match, were congratulated by the coach.

2 The players who had done their very best to win the match were congratulated by the coach.

Sentence 1 has commas around the subordinate clause '**who had done their very best to win the match**'; sentence 2 does not.

In the first sentence, the subordinate clause is a descriptive clause. It gives additional information about the players, **they had done their very best to win the match**, while in the second sentence, the subordinate clause **identifies or defines** which players are meant: only '**the players who had done their very best to win the match**' were congratulated by the coach. This sentence would be clearer if it said:

> The players <u>that</u> had done their very best to win the match were congratulated by the coach.

'That' instead of 'who' removes any confusion when the information is **defining** rather than additional.

Here are some more examples:

   3 The third goal, which Alan scored, meant they won the match.
   4 The third goal that Alan scored meant they won the match.

In sentence 3 '**which Alan scored**' adds additional information about the winning goal. It was scored by Alan. The other goals could have been scored by someone else.

In sentence 4 '**that Alan scored**' identifies the goal. Obviously Alan scored three goals in all, the third of which won the match.

   5 The children, who had blue eyes, were chosen for the play.
   6 The children that had blue eyes were chosen for the play.

Sentence 5 gives us more information about 'the children': they had blue eyes.

Sentence 6 defines or identifies which children were chosen for the play: those that had blue eyes.

Notice that a **descriptive** clause is usually introduced by '**which**' or '**who**' and can be divided off from the rest of the sentence by a pair of commas. A **defining** clause is usually introduced by '**that**' and has no commas.

✓ *Checkpoint A*

1 Read the following letter aloud. It is written, for the most part, without punctuation marks. Decide where capital letters and full stops should be inserted.

Dear Madam

  this is a letter to confirm the booking I made by telephone as discussed, I have agreed to rent the cottage in Scotland for one week the dates are from the 13th to the 20th of August

  I enclose a cheque for £100 this is the deposit for the booking I realise that the balance will be due one month before the rental begins

  I would very much appreciate detailed travel directions nearer the time I would also like to know exactly what the cottage contains I am not quite clear how close it is to the nearest village any further general information you can give me would be much appreciated

    Yours faithfully

    Edward Baines

    Edward Baines

2 Some of the following compound and complex sentences would be clearer if a comma was inserted. Decide where a comma would be helpful.

a) I like tea but she prefers coffee.

b) The MPs decided to vote for the measure and their constituents largely agreed with them.

c) The clients were offered an alternative holiday or they could have their money refunded.

d) The star denied she had ever said that but the journalist insisted she had.

e) The postman delivered the letters which came from abroad and Linda eagerly tore the envelopes open.

3 Which of these sentences define the subject of the sentence and which do not?

   a) Those dogs that had been found as strays were more likely to be put to sleep.

   b) The men that were angry and exhausted demanded an instant apology.

   c) The women, who were extremely well-qualified for the post, interviewed very well.

   d) The computer program that had been set up by Bob was accepted.

   e) The computer program, which had been set up by Bob, was accepted.

Activities 1 and 2

1 The following passage uses a number of interjections that require one or a pair of commas. There are also a number of adverbs placed at the start of sentences that should have a comma after them. Rewrite the passage and insert them in the appropriate position.

> Job-seekers naturally have to prepare themselves thoroughly for the job market. Unfortunately not everyone appreciates this fact. Of course if someone has had professional advice, he or she is aware of the importance of making a good impression. Appearance for example is very important. Sadly some applicants turn up for job interviews dressed most inappropriately.
>
> There is however no mystery about choosing the appropriate clothes. Obviously you should ask yourself what would suit the particular environment you are entering. It would not for instance be appropriate to turn up in a dull city suit if you were being interviewed say at a very trendy music shop. On the other hand sweater and jeans would be inappropriate for an interview at a bank or insurance company.

2 Rewrite the following complex sentences in which commas have been omitted, inserting them where you think appropriate.

   a) The exile returned home which delighted his parents who had not seen him for twenty years because he had emigrated to Australia all those years ago.

   b) Since the trend seemed to be upwards investors were drawn to invest in the Stock Market which had been going through a bad patch lately a development which had not surprised the experts because world markets were so depressed.

   c) Although the exam had been difficult most students felt they had done well enough to pass because they had been so well-prepared by their teacher whom they all admired.

CAPITAL LETTERS

Read the following article. Every time capital letters are used, they are numbered and underlined.

(1)When (2)I visited (3)The International Restaurant in (4)Preston Street, (5)I was greeted warmly at the door by (6)Jean Maloney, the co-owner. (7)That set the tone for the whole evening.

(8)My partner ordered melon with prawns in a special sauce, which she described as excellent, while for starters (9)I had smoked trout, again superb. For wine, we chose a (10)Cabernet Sauvignon.

(11)For my main course (12)I ordered veal (13)Normandy, which was cooked in cream and served with apples. (14)My companion had duck in orange sauce. (15)The sauce was a bit on the sweet side.

(16)For pudding we both had generous helpings of banoffee pie. (17)All in all, a superb meal.

(18)Mr (19)John Maloney, (20)Jean's husband, is the chef. (21)The International is open (22)Monday to (23)Saturday and for (24)Sunday lunch. (25)Bookings are now being taken for (26)Christmas lunch. (27)I thoroughly recommend this restaurant.

1   a capital letter is used at the start of a sentence

2   the first person singular, I, always has a capital letter

3   a proper noun, in this case, the name of a place or institution; note that all three words in the name have capital letters

4   an address; again both parts of the address have a capital letter

5   first person singular again

6   a proper noun, the name of a person; both names have a capital letter

7   capital letter at the beginning of a new sentence

8   capital letter at the start of a new paragraph and sentence

9   first person singular

10 the name of a specific product

11 new sentence

12 first person singular

13 a place name included in the title of a dish

14 new sentence

15 new sentence

16 new sentence

17 new sentence

18 new sentence, but also because of the title Mr

19 someone's name with both parts taking a capital letter

20 similarly for the first name

21 the name of the restaurant

22, 23 and 24 days of the week have capital letters

25 new sentence

26 festivals, such as Christmas, have capital letters

27 first person singular

Here are some reminders of other uses of capital letters:

It's a long, long time from May to December

'Cats' is adapted from T. S. Eliot's 'Old Possum's Book of Practical Cats'.

Dr Newman
3 Pryor Crescent
Broughton
East Sussex
DN1 6MO
England

The American President will meet the British Prime Minister next week at the White House

All my love
Aunt Beth

Dear Joe,

1 **Coronation Street**
2 **Neighbours**
3 **The Weakest Link**
4 **Match of the Day**

Among the most popular tourist attractions are the Tower of London, Edinburgh Castle, Madame Tussaud's and Windsor Castle.

She has worked for the UN, the EC, and the IMF.

✓ Checkpoint B

Read the following letter. Capital letters have been omitted. Decide where capital letters should have been used.

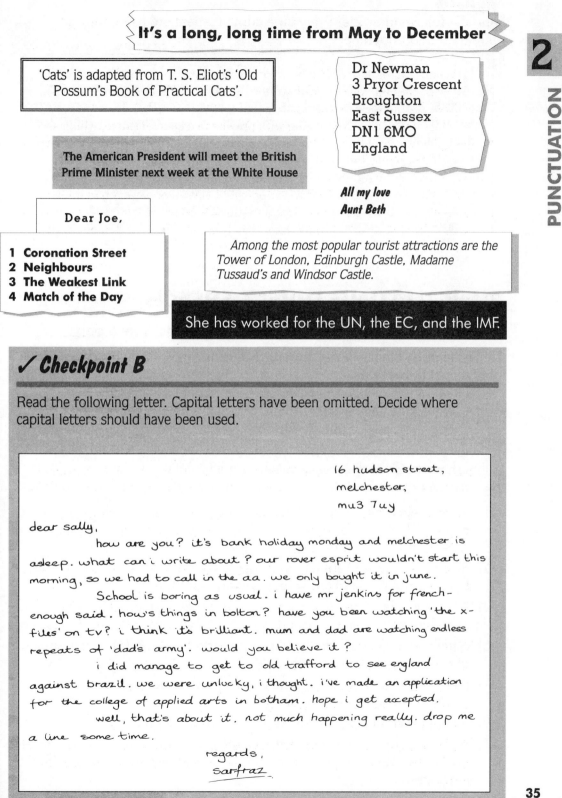

16 hudson street,
melchester,
mu3 7uy

dear sally,

how are you? it's bank holiday monday and melchester is asleep. what can i write about? our rover esprit wouldn't start this morning, so we had to call in the aa. we only bought it in june.

School is boring as usual. i have mr jenkins for french — enough said. how's things in bolton? have you been watching 'the x-files' on tv? i think it's brilliant. mum and dad are watching endless repeats of 'dad's army'. would you believe it?

i did manage to get to old trafford to see england against brazil. we were unlucky, i thought. i've made an application for the college of applied arts in botham. hope i get accepted.

well, that's about it. not much happening really. drop me a line some time.

regards,
sarfraz.

Activity 3

Read the following article. Again capital letters have been omitted. Rewrite the article inserting capital letters where appropriate.

'the dancing era', the new musical by andrew knox that opened at the lyric theatre last night, should delight mr knox's many admirers. With a book by tom brice and directed by sheila mayhew, the show has every chance of running in london for many a month. Its hit tune will be 'dancing mid the tulips', but other numbers, such as 'tripping the fantastic' and 'delight' should also please fans.

After its london run, the show is tipped for sydney, new york and paris. stuart mackenzie, the chief backer of the show, stated that lena bjorn, the star of the show, has been signed on a long-term contract. It should have earned its investment back by easter and by christmas it should have made millions in profit. 'This can only be good for british theatre,' said mr mackenzie.

PUNCTUATING DIRECT SPEECH

Look at the punctuation of direct speech in this extract from a story:

[1]'Remember, Ethan, this is a great chance for us [2,3]' said Rachel. [4]'We can't afford to botch it[5.6]'

[7 8]'I know that[9,10]' Ethan protested[11], [12]'[13]but I'm trying my best[14.15]'

[16 17]'But is your best good enough[18?19]' said Rachel caustically.

[20 21]'Hey[22,23]' said Ethan in a hurt tone[24], [25] '[26]what do you mean by that[27?28]'

In that short stretch of direct speech (where the actual words the characters in the story say are written down), there are numerous punctuation rules to note:

(1) open speech marks or inverted commas; you may use single inverted commas '   ', or double "   "; the first word after the opening speech marks requires a capital letter

(2) a comma is placed **inside** the closing speech marks (3), which come before what is called the **interruption**: said Rachel

(4) it is still the same speaker so a new paragraph is not required, but speech marks must be opened again, with a capital letter at the first word

(5) a full stop comes inside the closing inverted comma (6) as this stretch of direct speech comes to an end

(7) there is a new speaker so a new paragraph is needed, with inverted commas being opened again (8)

(9) a comma comes inside the closing inverted comma (10)

(11) there is a comma after the **interruption**, because the second half of this direct speech is still part of the same sentence that started with 'I know that'

(12) speech marks are opened again, but this time there is a lower case

letter at the first word (13), not a capital letter, because it is not a new sentence but a continuation of the sentence that comes before the interruption

(14) a full stop at the end of the speech and close inverted commas (15)

(16) a new paragraph because the speech has 'changed hands' again and open inverted commas (17)

(18) a question mark inside the closing inverted commas (19)

(20) a new paragraph, open inverted commas (21)

(22) a comma is placed inside the closing inverted commas (23)

(24) a comma after the interruption and before the sentence of speech is continued

(25) open inverted commas and a lower case letter at the first word (26) because it is still the same sentence which was started before the interruption

(27) a question mark inside the closing inverted commas (28).

It is essential that when you use direct speech in your writing, you make it clear who is speaking. Always start a new paragraph when a new speaker says something, even if there are only two speakers. Always place the punctuation mark that falls at the end of a stretch of direct speech just inside the closing inverted commas.

Another common error is to mix single and double inverted commas. If you use single ones at the start of a speech, use single ones at the end too. If you choose double ones, use them at the start and at the end.

For a more detailed explanation of the punctuation of direct speech, see Section 3 in *Basic Punctuation*.

Activity 4

Read the following passage. Direct speech has been used, but all punctuation marks have been omitted. Rewrite the passage inserting the correct punctuation.

let me see, let me see said the crazy inventor you want me to make a time machine is that right

exactly said Michael I want to travel into the future

that's easy the inventor said emphatically

if it is so easy said Michael why haven't you done it before now

no one has ever asked me to anyway I've been too busy with the present to bother with the future

but you will do it asked Michael

of course said the inventor I said I would and I will

when will you start you see I have to get into the future as soon as possible

you want it yesterday then joked the inventor don't be in such a hurry

I have a special reason for haste said Michael but I can't tell you about it

your reasons don't concern me replied the inventor but the challenge does

let's get on with it then said Michael time is getting on

COLONS AND SEMI-COLONS

- Sentences need a capital letter at the beginning and a punctuation mark at the end: that can be a full stop, a question mark or an exclamation mark.
- Sentences also frequently require commas to separate one unit of sense from another.
- In addition, however, there are times when you may use colons (:) and semi-colons (;).

A **colon** does not have the same 'strength' as a full stop, but it is 'stronger' than a comma or a semi-colon.

It is used frequently to introduce lists:

Scotland has four major cities: Glasgow, Edinburgh, Aberdeen and Dundee.

The following ingredients are absolutely essential: spring onions, garlic, salt, cornflour, chopped tomatoes, olive oil, baby carrots and tomato purée.

In both these examples, the list of items follows a simple sentence that makes sense on its own. The list consists of an explanation or amplification.

Note, too, that colons are frequently used to introduce quotations:

One of the most famous lines in movie history is the last line of 'Gone with the Wind': 'After all, tomorrow is another day.'

Sometimes the 'list' that a colon precedes is in the form of a few simple sentences:

> The reforms have three benefits: they are sweeping, they are popular and they will gain votes for the government.

There will be occasions in your own writing when it will be appropriate for you to use colons. If you are accurate in doing so, it will make your meaning much clearer to the reader.

Semi-colons may be used to separate two statements that are closely linked with one another. A semi-colon may take the place of a full stop and, by doing so, create a close link between two separate sentences.

Listen, Colon, as far as I'm concerned, you'll never be a full stop. And that goes for you too, Semi-colon.

Look at these examples:

> In England, the two national games are football and cricket. In America they are American football and baseball.

These two statements are expressed in two separate sentences. However, the two sentences are closely linked. So, an alternative way of punctuating them would be:

> In England, the two national games are football and cricket; in America they are American football and baseball.

The second statement is linked to the first and is of more or less equal importance, so it is appropriate that a semi-colon separates them. Notice that after a semi-colon, a lower case letter is correct unless, of course, the word requires a capital letter anyway.

Here are some more examples of the use of semi-colons:

> I like tea; she prefers coffee.
>
> The public loved the musical; the critics hated it.
>
> The groom was in morning dress; the guests wore lounge suits.

As these sentences make contrasting statements it is appropriate that a semi-colon should separate the two halves.

Sometimes, items in a list are described in several words. In this case semi-colons, rather than commas, should separate the items:

> The measures we propose are as follows: revenue should be raised by charging an admission fee; the museum should be closed on Mondays; several staff redundancies will have to be implemented; an advertising campaign to attract more visitors should be arranged.

The use of semi-colons between each lengthy item in this list emphasises the importance of each item and makes it easier for the reader to take in the information.

In your own writing, there will be opportunities to use semi-colons. Being able to use them correctly is a sign of 'punctuation competence'.

Activity 5

1 There are opportunities to use colons in the following examples. Rewrite each section, inserting colons appropriately.

a) I think this is the loveliest line that Shakespeare wrote. 'Shall I compare thee to a summer's day?'

b) These are the teams left in the draw for the next round of the cup. Blackburn, Chelsea, Bristol Rovers, Everton, Sunderland, Leeds and Tranmere Rovers.

c) For the best actor award, the following have been nominated. Robert de Niro, Tom Cruise, Tom Hanks, Jim Carrey and Gary Oldman.

d) The Brontë sisters wrote some of the best novels in the English language. 'Wuthering Heights', 'Jane Eyre' and 'Villette'.

2 Rewrite the following passage, inserting semi-colons where you think they would be appropriate.

Producing a competent curriculum vitae is essential for all job-seekers. A CV should not only give essential information. It should also represent the applicant in a favourable light. Among the features of an impressive CV are the following: neatness of presentation and logical organisation of material, accuracy of spelling, punctuation and grammar, a detailed account of the applicant's previous history, a clear and concise list of previous work experience, an accurate account of relevant educational qualifications, the willingness to give an impression of the applicant's personality and interests.

THE USE OF THE APOSTROPHE

The apostrophe is frequently misused in written English.

One of the most common mistakes is to confuse **'its'** and **'it's'**.

Here are alternative versions of a newspaper headline:

IT'S A GIRL!

ITS A GIRL!

The first heading is the correct one: **'it's'** is the contracted form of **it is**, so, therefore, an apostrophe marks the missing **i**. In the second headline, **'its'** has been incorrectly used; **its** without an apostrophe means 'belonging to it'.

Here is another example of a newspaper headline:

The Budget and Its Implications for You

This time 'its' has been used correctly, because it means 'belong to it'.

Confusing **it's** and **its** is a bad error. Make sure you understand when each one is used. Do not use 'it's' when the meaning is 'belonging to it', although, as we are about to see, all other cases of ownership do have an apostrophe.

Another common fault is to insert apostrophes in straightforward plurals. This is another bad error. Apostrophes are only used with nouns to indicate ownership:

1 my friend's house   2 the team's jerseys   3 the politicians' excuses

In 1, the apostrophe indicates ownership of the house by **'my friend'**. *Friend* is singular so the apostrophe comes before the *s*.

In 2, **'team'** is a collective noun (there is one team), so it is treated as singular. Once more, the apostrophe comes before the *s*.

In 3, the apostrophe comes after the *s*, because **'politicians'** is a plural noun and to indicate ownership, plural nouns have the apostrophe after the final letter.

However, look at this incorrect use of apostrophes in words that are plurals not indicating ownership of any kind:

My friends' live in a very comfortable house.

The team's clearly did not like one another.

The politicians' gave all kinds of excuses.

In these examples, the plural version of nouns have been given apostrophes incorrectly. The correct versions of these sentences are:

My friends live in a very comfortable house.

The teams clearly did not like one another.

The politicians gave all kinds of excuses.

Inserting unnecessary apostrophes in plurals is a fairly common error. Avoid it. Ask yourself whether you are indicating **ownership**. If you are, you should use an apostrophe. If you are not, then use the straightforward plural. (The only exception to this rule is 'its'.)

Activity 6

There are numerous errors in the use of **it's** and **its** in the following report. In addition, some apostrophes have been incorrectly inserted in plurals, while there are also places where apostrophes should have been used to indicate ownership. Rewrite the passage putting these errors right.

Its not really that surprising that the United Nation's has lost much of its authority. It's authority only comes from the effort's that the various member nations' make to add to the organisations credibility.

Sadly, the interests of the individual countries' usually come before those of the UN. Its a fact that some member's preach co-operation among the nation's of the world, but practise power politic's. The UN depends on the goodwill of it's members'; its reputation is only as high as that of it's member state's.

War's cannot be prevented by the United Nations. It's primary functions are to reconcile enemies' and to provide mean's of helping impoverished areas' of the world. Its a great pity that the basic belief's of it's charter seem to have been forgotten by it's most prominent supporters'.

SKILLCHECK Check these statements to assess what you have learnt from this chapter. If you cannot honestly tick all of these statements, then go back over the relevant section.

❑ I understand that punctuation aids clarity and comprehension.

❑ I understand how to punctuate sentences and how to recognise where one sentence ends and another begins.

❑ I am confident about using semi-colons and colons.

❑ I know how to avoid mistakes in using the apostrophe.

3
WRITING IN PARAGRAPHS

- Paragraphs are a means of organising written material for the benefit of you, the writer, and for those who read what you write.

- A paragraph may be thought of as a unit of meaning within a longer piece of writing.

- To be a unit, it has to deal with content that is connected and that is structured within the paragraph.

- Each paragraph should follow on from, and be linked to, the previous paragraph and the one that follows.

SETTING OUT PARAGRAPHS

There are two ways of 'setting out' paragraphs on the page.

■ INDENTED PARAGRAPHS

In most handwritten material, paragraphs are shown by **indenting** the first line of each paragraph.

> In my opinion, there is no substitute for a good melody. The trouble with most modern music is the lack of a tune. In fact, I would go so far as to say that that is what music is essentially about : melody.
>
> Consider the art of story-telling. What is a story without a strong story-line? The narrative art depends on creating memorable plots. Just as novels. . . . .

Indent about a centimetre from the left-hand margin. Make the indentation clear and consistent for each new paragraph you write, so that your reader is in no doubt that you are starting a new paragraph.

■ BLOCK PARAGRAPHS

A different format for paragraphing is used in many formal letters. This alternative format is called **block paragraphing**. New paragraphs are not indicated by indenting from the margin. Each paragraph is separated from the other by a line space. The paragraphs appear as 'blocks' on the page.

Note the 'block' format of the layout of this letter. In addition, there is none of the usual punctuation that you would include in the opening and closing of a handwritten letter. There will be more about letter writing in Part B of this book.

Dear Madam

We apologise for the delay in the delivery of the curtains you have ordered. We realise that this has caused you some inconvenience which we very much regret.

This delay has been caused by factors outside our direct control. The suppliers of our curtain material have informed us that they are waiting for delivery of the particular colour you have requested. They hope to have delivery within two weeks.

Rest assured that, once we have received the material from the suppliers, the curtains will be made up straightaway. Once again, please accept our apologies for the delay.

Yours faithfully

S. Lock.

S. Lock

WHAT IS A PARAGRAPH?

A paragraph should deal with one aspect of the topic you are writing about. A paragraph is a way of focusing on one aspect of a topic by making a statement about it and developing that point within the paragraph.

It is useful to think in terms of using a **key** or **topic** sentence as the first sentence of each paragraph. This key or topic sentence communicates to your reader what the paragraph will be about.

This does **not** mean you write something like 'In this paragraph I am going to discuss . . .'. It means you make a concise statement, probably in the form of a simple sentence.

> The effects of the economic recession have been disastrous for the car industry.

This concise statement indicates to the reader what this paragraph will be about. This first sentence of the paragraph is the **key** sentence, from which the rest of the paragraph will develop.

Indeed, your reader is entitled to expect that you will expand on the point you have made in this opening key sentence. Look at the complete paragraph:

> 1 The effects of the economic recession have been disastrous for the car industry.   2 Manufacturing output has fallen and the level of investment drastically reduced.   3 Inevitably, this has meant that the numbers employed in manufacturing have steadily fallen during the recession.
> 4 It is, perhaps, difficult to see how the industry can ever recover its former position in world terms.

Sentence 1 is the key sentence of the paragraph.

Sentence 2 gives examples of, or illustrates, the effects of the recession.

Sentence 3 expands this point and gives a further example.

Sentence 4 makes a point about the long-term effect on the industry. This final sentence has a 'summarising' function in the paragraph and puts the initial point made in the key sentence in a wider context.

Thus, a useful paragraph structure to follow would be:

- a key or topic sentence
- a development of the point in one or more sentences, including examples that illustrate the particular point, or giving a more detailed explanation
- a closing sentence that somehow gathers together the content of the paragraph.

This paragraph structure would be appropriate for all kinds of written English. For example, look at the paragraph overleaf that someone has written in a report about work experience:

On the whole, I consider the experience I gained was of major benefit to me. I saw the working of a bank from the inside. I got a taste of what it will be like to work on a day-to-day basis. In addition, it gave me an insight into the problems that come with serving the general public. The experience has helped me think about how I should prepare myself for the job market.

The paragraph opens with a key sentence that indicates what the particular topic of the paragraph will be. The next three sentences illustrate the benefits the writer gained from the experience. The closing sentence presents a conclusion about the longer-term benefits of the experience.

In your own writing, think about the structure of the paragraphs you write. The format we have suggested is a useful guideline for you to follow.

✓ Checkpoint A

The following newspaper report has been printed without paragraphs. Read the passage through and decide where you think new paragraphs should be started.

Hampton councillors will be asked at the next council meeting to approve the construction of a new leisure centre in Eastern Road. This is one of the options Hampton's Sports and Entertainment Officer, John Jones, will recommend to the Leisure Committee. The construction will result in the closing of the temporary car park. The majority of residents in the Eastern Road area who responded to the recent questionnaire circulated to householders by the council supported the changes. Residents claimed the leisure centre would improve the image of the area. The resulting traffic increase was of much less consequence. Indeed, a sizeable proportion of residents recommended that residents' parking should be introduced and the leisure centre should have an underground car park. However, the Sports and Entertainment Officer says this would not be feasible. His recommendations about parking facilities is a suitable compromise, he claims.

Activity 1

Below are some key or topic sentences. Make each of them the first sentence of a paragraph about the topic that is indicated in this sentence. Structure each paragraph according to the advice given above.

a) Drug addiction is a growing problem among young people in many countries nowadays.

b) The introduction of a national lottery has been a major success.

c) Job satisfaction is equally as important as salary in choosing a career.

d) Equal opportunities for men and women must be a feature of the workplace.

CONTINUITY

We have emphasised the need to write coherent paragraphs that hang together.

Equally important is the need to link paragraphs together so that there is a 'flow' to your writing.

If a piece of writing consists of seemingly unconnected paragraphs, then it will appear disjointed and incoherent. It is your job to provide 'signposts' for your readers so they can see the direction your argument is taking.

Careful planning before you start writing will help enormously in organising your material. Always spend a few minutes before you write anything of any length making some notes and a brief outline.

In the writing of the piece, you should be aware of the need to provide links between the paragraphs you have written.

You can use linking words and phrases that help provide just the kind of continuity your writing needs. Look at this example:

> Computer literacy is becoming a 'must' for most office workers these days. So much information is now stored in computer files that a person who is not adept at retrieving and storing information on computer files is at a real disadvantage.
>
> However, educational establishments are now fully aware of this development. They are geared to train students to understand computer language and technology. It is the older generation who are missing out.
>
> Nevertheless, many records are still kept in paper form. Finding essential information from old-fashioned files can be costly in terms of time and the space these files take up, but some people will always be wedded to traditional ways.
>
> On the other hand . . .

In this example the linking words or phrases that have been used are:

however   nevertheless   on the other hand

These linking words help give the passage continuity and coherence, and make it easier for the reader to follow the argument.

Here are some other words or phrases that you may use to help link your paragraphs:

in addition   additionally   this (the demonstrative pronoun)   that
on the contrary   by contrast   equally   another factor   firstly
secondly   despite this fact   yet   also   similarly   the next   fortunately
unfortunately   sadly   happily   hence   therefore   thus   in conclusion
lastly   finally

Activities 2 and 3

2 Read the following passage. Decide where you think new paragraphs should begin and use appropriate linking words or phrases to give greater continuity to the passage.

Performing well at a job interview is dependent on numerous factors. You must make sure you arrive in plenty of time for the appointment. You do not want to appear flustered and out-of-breath because you have had to rush to get there. Making the right impression through your appearance is a plus. No one will be impressed if someone turns up for an important interview badly dressed or looking scruffy. Give some thought to what you will wear and what would be appropriate. During the interview, try to make direct eye contact with the particular person who is asking you questions. There is nothing worse than looking at an interviewee who is gazing at the floor or around the room. Good eye contact is a sign that you are honest and sincere. Clarity of speech and thought before answering is an obvious advantage. Most people are nervous during interviews. It is best to acknowledge that and then conquer it. With the best will in the world, interviewers cannot give credit to applicants who mumble or freeze. Try to avoid appearing dogmatic in your views. You must make the interviewing panel think you will be able to co-operate with your colleagues. You must have some views of your own. No one wants to employ an individual without real personality. It is a tricky balance to get right.

3 Write a short piece on any of the following, dividing your writing up into appropriate paragraphs and employing linking words or phrases.

a) the example set by sporting stars to young people

b) the cult of violence in the cinema

c) do we live in a celebrity culture?

4
SPELLING

- **Spelling matters. That is the first thing to grasp about this aspect of written English.**

- **Don't accept the idea that inaccurate spelling does not 'spoil' what you write. It does. When you put anything into written form, you are communicating an impression of yourself to other people. If what you write is full of spelling errors, then it is bound to be noticed.**

- **Another false idea about spelling is that you can't do anything about being a 'bad speller'. People say, 'I've never been able to spell!' and shrug their shoulders as though there is nothing to be done. This is not true, but improved spelling accuracy takes hard work, attention to detail and perseverance.**

SPELLING RULES?

English spelling is full of irregularities, so it is difficult to talk about 'spelling rules' as such. However, there are some general patterns that you should be aware of.

The rane in Spane fals manely in the plane.

No, no, darling! The <u>rain</u> in <u>Spain</u> <u>falls</u> <u>mainly</u> in the <u>plain</u>!

- **'i' before 'e' except after 'c'**

  This rule applies only to words where the vowel sound is 'ee':

  achieve   believe   chief   diesel   relieve   wield   ceiling   conceive
  deceive   receive

  But there are many exceptions:

  counterfeit   seize   weird   species

  Words with 'ei' that is not pronounced 'ee' are not affected by this rule:

  deign   feign   reign

- **'c' in the noun, 's' in the verb**

  A few words have a 'c' in the noun and an 's' in the verb. The most common example of this is 'practice' and 'practise':

  The practice started at six o'clock.
  We had to practise for our music exams.

  Other examples: prophecy/prophesy   licence/license

PLURALS

- **Words ending in 'y'**

  These generally form their plural by dropping the 'y' and adding 'ies':

  ally → allies   army → armies   caddy → caddies   dairy → dairies
  fairy → fairies   lady → ladies   story → stories

  However, words that have a 'y' after a vowel (a, e, i, o, u), retain the final 'y' and add 's':

  chimney → chimneys   boy → boys   donkey → donkeys

- **Words ending in 's', 'ss', 'x', 'sh' and 'ch'**

  These form their plural by adding 'es':

  bus → buses   dress → dresses   box → boxes   wish → wishes
  church → churches

- **Words ending in 'o'**

  These generally add 'es' to form their plural:

  tomato → tomatoes   potato → potatoes   echo → echoes
  cargo → cargoes   hero → heroes

  However, there are important exceptions:
  piano → pianos   photo → photos

- **Words ending in 'f'**

  Some words ending in 'f' form their plural by replacing the 'f' with a 'v' and adding 'es':

  calf → calves   half → halves   knife → knives   leaf → leaves
  loaf → loaves   thief → thieves

  But other words ending in 'f' form their plural in the regular way:

  roof → roofs   proof → proofs   handkerchief → handkerchiefs

- **Nouns ending in 'our'**

  Nouns ending in 'our' drop the 'u' when the adjective is formed:

  humour → humorous   glamour → glamorous   vigour → vigorous

  An exception is honour → honourable

- **Adjectives ending in 'ful', 'al' and 'ic'**

  Adjectives ending in 'ful' (note that it is a single 'l', not a double 'l' in these adjectives) form adverbs by adding 'ly':

  careful → carefully   beautiful → beautifully   doubtful → doubtfully
  resourceful → resourcefully

  Similarly, adjectives ending in 'al' form adverbs by adding 'ly':

  accidental → accidentally   actual → actually   critical → critically
  real → really

  Adjectives ending in 'ic' add 'ally' to form adverbs:

  basic → basically   acerbic → acerbically   demonic → demonically
  fantastic → fantastically   terrific → terrifically

- **Words ending in 'ic'**

  These verbs add a 'k' before 'ing' or 'ed'

  picnic → picnicked   panic → panicking   mimic → mimicked

SOME COMMON ERRORS

Below are some common spelling errors that should be avoided.

- **their/there/they're**

  Never mistake **their** for **there** and vice versa:

  Their train was late.   Their parents met them.   Their story is a fascinating one.

  All these examples use **their** correctly to mean 'belonging to them'.

  There is only one solution.   The perfume department is over there.
  There exists a master plan to conquer the planet.

In these examples, **there** either draws attention to the fact that something is or exists, or means 'in that place'.

They're all we have left.   They're my cousins.

They're is the contracted form of **they are**.

- **were/where/we're**

Similarly, these three words are sometimes confused with each other.

We were going about our business.   Where were you last night?

Where do you think you're going?   I don't know where to go from here.

We're in the money. We're not getting any younger.

SPELLING LIST

Below is a list of common words in alphabetical order. You should be able to spell all these words correctly. Learn a few every day. Using them will help you remember them. If you are not sure what any of them mean, look them up in a dictionary.

absence accelerate accept accidentally accommodation ache achievement acknowledge acquaintance acquire address advertisement affect agreeable aid aisle album alcohol alive allege alliance ally almost aloof already altogether always amount analysis ancestors animal annoyed answer appalling apparatus apparently appear appearance applause appropriate argument arrived article artificial assembly associate assume assumption attitude aunt author autumn avoid awful awkward

badge balloon banner barrier barrow basically beautiful because become beginning behave behaviour belief believe benefit benefited between bicycle biological board bored bridge build building burglar buried bury business button

cabbage calendar calm campaign capable capital capture career careful carefully carriage carried catalogue caution ceiling century championship channel chaos character chatted check cheerfully cheque cherish chief childhood children chocolate chord choreography Christmas chronic chronicle cigarette circuit coffee coil collaborate collar college colossal colour comfortable comical commission committee comparatively comparison competent completely computer conceive concerned condemn confusion conscience conscientious conscious consensus consistent conspiracy contemporary continually copper corporation correct corridor cottage courageous courteous criticism cruel culpable cupboard curiosity current cynical cynicism

deceit decision defence defensive definite delicious description despair desperately detached deteriorate deterred developed

difference   different   dilemma   disappearance   disappointing
disastrous   discipline   discouraged   disguise   disillusioned   disservice
dissolve   division   dreadful   dreadfully   duel

ecological   ecstasy   eerie   effort   eighth   electricity   elegant
embarrassment   endeavour   enormous   environment   essential
exaggerate   examination   exceed   except   exceptionally   excitement
exclaimed   excursion   exempt   exercise   exhausted   exhibition
exhilarating   existence   expedition   expense   experience   explanation
extraordinary   extravagant   extremely

family   fantastically   favourite   feasible   February   feud   fiery
financial   followed   foreign   fortunately   forty   fourteen   friend   fruit
fuel   fulfil   furniture

gauge   generous   gnaw   gorgeous   government   gracious   gradually
grammar   gripped   grotesque   guarantee   guard   guilt   guitar

half   halves   handkerchief   happened   harass   harbour   heaven
height   heir   hero   heroes   hideous   honesty   honour   honourable
howl   humorous   humour   hungrily   hurried   hygiene   hypocrisy

identical   identity   illegible   immediately   imminent   impossible
impudence   incidentally   incredible   independence   infinite   ingenious
initial   innocence   innocent   install   instalment   intellectual
intelligence   intention   interested   intrigue   invention   invincible
invisible   irrelevant   irresistible   island

jealous   jewellery/jewelry   junction   junior

keenness   knack   knew   knit   knob   know   knowledge
knowledgeable

laboratory   laid   language   lawyer   league   leaves   lecture   leisure
liaison   library   lieutenant   lightning   likelihood   literature   loathsome
logical   loneliness   luxury

magical   maintain   maintenance   majority   management   manoeuvre
manufacture   marriage   marvellous   material   mechanically   medicine
menial   miniature   miracle   miscellaneous   mission   musical
mysterious   mystifying

naturally   necessary   negligent   negotiate   neighbour   noticeable
nuisance   numerous

obstacle   obviously   occasionally   occurred   occurrence   offence
offend   offered   omission   operation   opportunity   ordinarily
ordinary   oxygen

paragraph   parallel   passion   patience   payment   pension
periodically   phase   philosophy   photograph   physical   picturesque
popular   possessions   practical   precious   preferred   pregnant
prejudice   preparation   prepare   preserve   pressure   pretence

SPELLING

privilege   probably   procedure   proceed   procession   produce
professional   profit   programme   prohibit   pronounce   proof
propaganda   property   prophet   proportion   protection   prove
psychology   puncture   pursue   pyjamas

quantity   quarrel   quarrelled   query   queue   quietly   quite   quota

really   receipt   receive   reception   recipe   recommend   referee
reference   referred   regional   relieved   religious   repetition
resistance   responsibility   restaurant   rhyme   rhythm   ridiculous
route   ruin

satellite   Saturday   scale   scarcely   scenery   scent   schedule
scheme   scholar   science   scientific   scissors   scratch   secretary
seemed   seize   selection   sentence   separate   serial   signal
silhouette   similar   similarly   sincerely   skilful   soldier   solicitor
souvenir   spectacles   statistics   stomach   storeys   stories   strolled
subtle   subtly   succeed   successful   successfully   suffered   sufficient
suggestion   summer   superstitious   surprising   survivor   suspicious
swallow   sympathy   system   systematic

taste   technical   technique   temperature   temporary   tendency
terrifying   thinner   thorough   threaten   threshold   thrift   thrilling
thrust   thwarted   tobacco   tolerance   tomorrow   tongue   touching
tragedy   tragic   tranquil   transistor   travel   travelled   tremendous
tries   triumph   tropical   truant   truly   twelfth   typical   tyranny

unbecoming   unbelievable   uncontrolled   unconventional   undeniable
underdeveloped   underneath   underrate   understanding   undoubtedly
unnecessary   unnerving   until   unusual   upsetting   usual

vacuum   vague   valley   valuable   vehicle   veil   velocity   vicious
vinegar   vision   visit   visitor   voice

weather   Wednesday   weekend   weight   weird   welcome   whether
wholesome   wilful   withhold   worry   wound

yacht   yawn   yearn   yeast   yellow   yield   young

zephyr   zero   zinc   zodiac   zone   zoom

A WORD ABOUT SPELLCHECKS

Word processors have become very common in offices and in homes. All sorts of software are manufactured as additional resources for users of word processors.

A **spellcheck** is a software program (usually part of a word-processing package) that you install into your computer to enable you to check the spelling of anything you have written.

A spellcheck is a very useful tool. Even accurate spellers can be blind to errors on a computer screen and find it much easier to pick out any mistakes in the printed version.

A spellcheck will scan the text and draw your attention to wrongly spelt words. It will also offer you the correct spelling.

However, a word of warning. Spellchecks are only capable of picking up misspelt or repeated words. If a word has been spelt correctly, but is, in fact, the 'wrong' word for a particular context, the spellcheck will not highlight it for you.

We <u>where</u> late for the meeting.

In this example, 'where' will be read by most spellchecks as correctly spelt because it is the word 'where', associated with place.

However, the sentence should read:

We <u>were</u> late for the meeting.

Another example of this would be:

She said the shop was over <u>their</u>.

In this example, 'their' is the wrong word (it should be 'there'), but as it is a correctly spelt word, the spellcheck will almost certainly not draw your attention to it.

Therefore, although spellchecks are very useful, they cannot do the whole job for you.

The most effective policy is to use the spellcheck to check what you have written on a word processor before you print it off and then read it carefully yourself to make sure that 'wrong' words have not slipped into the text.

There is no real substitute for being able to spell yourself. Being dependent on software does not make you 'spellproof'.

Activities 1 and 2

1 Read the following passage. Several words have been misspelt. Rewrite the passage correcting these errors.

It was during the riegn of George II that the Jacobites made there last cerious attempt to sieze the throne. Charles Edward Stuart, none as the Young Pretender, landed on the west cost of Scotland in 1745, and was wellcomed by the chieves of powerfull clans. Bonnie Prince Charlie, usally portrayed as a glamourous figure in fiction and films, was, in fact, a week and vacilating man, who found it difficult to comunicate with his genrals because of his inadequate English. However, the rebelion started promisingly when the Jacobite armys where granted entry into Edinburgh without a fight.

2 Rewrite the following letter, correcting any spelling errors.

Dear Sir

Nowadays were subjected, more and more, to noise levels that would of been quite unacceptible a few years ago. I am certin that any politicle party that made a plege to impose bans on unecesary noise in public places would gane in popularity.

Their seams to be no ceiling on the level of noise that is acceptable in hour society. Walkmans, motor bikes, rode drils and car horns are only a few of the iritations that can plague our streets. Frequently, won reads about neighbors coming to blows or going to court becos of the noise inflicted on one party by anuther. Were will it all end? Let's face it: were a nation of noisy louts. Curtesy seems to have gone from our way of live.

Yours faithfully

A. Grudge.

Alfred Grudge

SKILLCHECK   Check these statements to assess what you have learnt from this chapter. If you cannot honestly tick all of these statements, then go back over the relevant section.

❏ I understand the need for accurate spelling.

❏ I realise that English spelling is frequently 'irregular', but that some rules or patterns are useful to know.

❏ I have learnt how to spell the words in the list provided.

PART B
ENGLISH AT WORK

INTRODUCTION

- **Most formal written English is in Standard English.**
- **Standard English is the kind of English that you hear mostly on the radio and television in news bulletins, 'serious' programmes, such as documentaries, and anything, indeed, with an 'official' or academic slant.**
- **In written form, Standard English is used in official documents, indeed in most formal written communications of all kinds, and in the language used by government, both local and national.**
- **In the world of work also, almost all written material uses Standard English, as in the following staff notice:**

Staff Notice

As is customary, the works will be closed for the festive season between 24 December and 1 January inclusive. Employees will be expected back at work promptly on 2 January. May the management take this opportunity to wish all staff a happy and prosperous New Year.

Most of us use much less formal English than this, particularly in everyday speech, when we are among our family and friends or in informal situations. Most people's spoken English also includes words and structures which are typical of their own local 'dialect' or form of English. This is entirely appropriate in informal situations, but it is not suited to more formal situations and that means most written communications, for practical reasons. Many local dialects are not immediately understood outside the area in which they are spoken, and informal English can be unclear as well as unsuitable in a situation where you have to communicate with official bodies, for example. To communicate clearly in written English, you must, therefore, use Standard English.

5

COMMUNICATIONS: LETTERS, MEMOS, NOTES, FAXES AND E-MAILS

FORMAL AND INFORMAL WRITING

Look at these extracts from different types of letters:

Dear Ali,
How's it going then? Things are great this end. I'm off on holiday soon to Wales and I'm looking forward to that, you bet! School is really a pain at the moment with the mock exams etc. Got the new Jam CD at the weekend- excellent!...

Dear Louise,
It was good to see you at the conference last week and make contact again after all these years. You certainly seem to have made a success of your new job and it was interesting to share views about the current trends.
I am really looking forward to working with you next month. This letter is about the possibility of our arranging a meeting before next month's event, so that we can talk about strategies. I can offer the following dates...

3

> Dear Sir
>
> We are writing about the non-payment of the invoice sent to you on 24 February last in connection with building works carried out by our firm. The invoice clearly states that payment is expected within one calendar month. However, two months have now elapsed and no settlement of the amount has been forthcoming.
>
> Unless we have payment within the next fourteen days, we regret we will have to . . .

Letter 1 is quite informal in tone and language, because it is a personal letter to a friend. The informal English used is **appropriate** for the purpose and context of this letter.

Letter 2 is more formal than letter 1, but it has personal touches, because it is a letter between business colleagues who have seen each other recently and know each other quite well. Yet, it is quite businesslike in tone and it does not use the kind of informal expressions used in the first letter.

Letter 3 is very formal in tone, because of the content and the purpose behind the communication. Unlike letters 1 and 2, it is highly impersonal so the tone and language are **appropriate** for the purpose.

Remember, an informal, personal, 'chatty' tone and language may be appropriate for many letters and other kinds of written communications (memos, notes), but for most written communications to people other than individuals you know very well, it is appropriate to use a semi-formal (letter 2) or a formal (letter 3) tone. The level of formality in tone and language is also called the **register**.

Read the following letters. Decide how informal or formal they are in terms of their tone and language. How would you describe their tone: very informal, informal, semi-formal, formal or very formal?

a)

Dear Max

It was a good meeting with you the other day and we must have lunch soon. I was very interested in your ideas for new business and I would certainly like to swap ideas. Why don't you fax me some of your's and I'll do the same this end?

I hope your holiday recharges your batteries and that you'll come back full of ideas to make lots of money.

Best wishes

Reg

Reg

b)

Dear Madam

It has come to our notice that our bill sent to you on 6 June last is still outstanding. We request that you make payment without delay or we may be forced to recover the amount through legal action.

Yours faithfully

J. Dalrymple

J. Dalrymple
General Manager

5

COMMUNICATIONS

c)

Hi, Ben!

How's it going? Here it's really boring, know what I mean? I'm desperately looking forward to the concert The Grunge are giving next week. D'you think we could get the lead guitarist's autograph?

Till then, all the best. Can't wait for the concert. See you.

Jackie

d)

Dear Ms Reid

I am writing to enquire whether there is the possibility of part-time work in your department. I am experienced in several aspects of the clothing industry and can furnish details of relevant past experience.

I would want to work for no more than twenty hours a week. I am available for interview at any time. I look forward to hearing from you.

Yours sincerely

Rachel Jackson.

Rachel Jackson

MORE ABOUT LETTER WRITING

The layout of a letter varies according to the degree of formality of the particular letter you are writing.

For example, if you are writing a letter to a personal friend or relative, there is less formality in the layout:

17 Acacia Avenue,
Bottlesham,
BJ1 3TR

16 February 2005

Dear Jenny,
      I hope...

All the best,
Sammy .

The points to note here are:

- the address and date at the top right-hand corner of the letter
- the absence of the addressee's name and address above the greeting 'Dear Jenny'
- the informal closing greeting 'All the best'
- the signature 'Sammy'.

Now look at this next letter in terms of its layout.

INDEPENDENT BUILDING SERVICES

15 ROTHMERE STREET

RADLINGTON RT2 9UL

16 February 2005

Mrs R. Jacobs
Personnel Director
Chambers and Sons
57 Tyburn Lane
Straunton
SY5 7YH

Dear Ruth

I am writing to remind you of the meeting we have arranged for March 8th at the Straunton Conference Centre in the Salisbury Room. I am very pleased that we have managed to clear time to have this meeting and I . . .

Best regards

Yours sincerely

James Lees

James Lees (Director of Training)

The points to note about this layout are:

- most business firms use 'headed paper' for letters, with the name of the firm and the address at the top of the letter
- the date is placed in the usual right-hand corner or on the left above the addressee's name and address
- the addressee's name and status in the firm are given and then the full address
- an informal greeting is used, because the writer knows the addressee well
- a 'block' format is being used, so there is no indenting from the edge of the paper
- it is common practice to include a more personal closing such as 'Best regards' when the two people know each other well, but there is also the more formal closing of 'Yours sincerely'
- the signature of the writer is followed by his name and position printed below it.

Now look at this third example, which also uses a 'block paragraphing' format:

PLANNING DEPARTMENT
Hilton County Council
Roberts Way
Hilton HJ1 6FG

16th February 2004

Occupant
45 Fryer Road
Hilton HJ2 3FF

Dear Sir/Madam

As you will know, the Hilton County Council are planning to construct a by-pass that will ease traffic congestion in the Surrenden area of the town. This letter is to inform you that work will commence on . . .

Yours faithfully

Delia Entwhistle

Delia Entwhistle
Director of Planning

The points to note about this layout are:

- the headed paper and the date above the addressee's name and address: in block formats, the date may appear in this place
- the addressee's name and address are not punctuated by commas or full stops
- the formal greeting 'Dear Sir/Madam' with no comma after it
- the closing is 'Yours faithfully' rather than 'Yours sincerely' because the addressee has not been addressed by name; no comma after 'faithfully'
- the signature and then the name and position of the writer.

Activity 1

Each of the following letters is written in an **inappropriate tone and language** for its purpose. Rewrite each of them using a different and appropriate tone and language.

a)

Dear Dorothy,

        It has come to my attention that you will be present at my party on Saturday the eighth of March next at the hour of 7.30. I am pleased to inform you that your presence will be welcome at this event and my respective parents are also anticipating your attendance with positive feelings. Please do not consider coming bearing gifts of any kind. Your presence will be sufficient.

        Yours faithfully,

Sylvia Magnus

     Sylvia Magnus

b)

Dear Mr Wilson,

        How are you then? Remember me? I worked in your firm's stores last summer holidays. Well, the fact is I've left school now and I thought I'd just drop you a line to ask if you've got anything going for me on, like, a permanent basis. Nothing too strenuous, of course!

        Frankly, I want to get a job to earn some cash. I want to go skiing at Christmas. Can you help out? Joking apart, I'd consider anything. See you then.

        Yours etc. *Rodney*

c)

Dear Madam,

        Thanks a lot for your recent order. I'm afraid we're having some difficulty with the old suppliers again. Can't help it at our end, but that sounds like excuses. We'll try and sort it out as soon as possible, depend on it. Look, immediately we get the stuff in, we'll rush it to you. O.K.? Be in touch.

        Best regards,

Laura

PARAGRAPHING LETTERS

We have already given examples of alternative formats in the layout of letters: the block format and the 'traditional' format.

Whatever format is used for the layout, a letter still has to be divided up into paragraphs. The advice about paragraphing we gave in Chapter 3 of Part A of this book is relevant to letter writing as well.

Look at the example below.

Dear Sir/Madam,

        I regret that I am returning the set of CDs that I ordered recently through your advertisement in the 'Express'. You dispatched the goods to me on 5th of October and the invoice number is CS1235.

        The reason I am returning the discs is because I am unable to play them on my CD player. The laser constantly 'slips' so that whole tracks are missed out. This is consistent in all three discs. I have played other CDs on my machine and I have had no problem with those. The fault clearly lies with the CDs you supplied.

        In these circumstances, I am asking for a complete refund of the money I paid for the discs. I would not be willing to accept replacement discs, because I am not confident that the same problem would not occur again. I hope to hear from you in the very near future.

        Yours faithfully,

Doug McGinty

        D. McGinty

An analysis of the structure of the letter shows that:

- paragraph 1 explains the purpose of the letter and gives essential information: details of the goods, the date of dispatch and the invoice number
- paragraph 2 gives more details relevant to the subject of the letter: the exact faults in the goods supplied
- paragraph 3 informs the addressee what the writer wants done and ends the letter with a request for a speedy reply.

In general terms, this paragraph structure is relevant to many types of formal letters:

- an opening paragraph: setting out the purpose of the letter and giving essential references and information
- development: one **or more** paragraphs developing the points you have made in the opening paragraph and going into more detail
- a closing paragraph: rounding off the letter, and pointing out what the writer wants the addressee to do.

Look at this further example; this time a block paragraphing format is used.

Dear Sir

Thank you for your letter of 14 October. We regret that the CDs we sent you in connection with our special offer proved faulty. We have dispatched a considerable number of these and very few have been returned to us as unsatisfactory in any way.

However, as you are dissatisfied with the goods, we will refund the full purchase price. In due time, our accounts department will be writing to you.

Once again please accept our apologies for the faulty CDs. I hope that this experience will not deter you from taking advantage of any future offers we make through the pages of the national press.

Yours faithfully

Jane Snow

Jane Snow (Assistant Marketing Manager)

The structure of this letter is as follows:

- paragraph 1 acknowledges the addressee's letter and apologises for the sending of faulty goods
- paragraph 2 explains what the firm intends to do in compensation
- paragraph 3 closes the letter appropriately.

When you are writing semi-formal or formal letters, you should follow this basic paragraphing structure.

It may be that some letters will require a longer 'middle section' of more than one paragraph.

All letters, however, should have a beginning, a middle and an end.

Activity 2

Read the following letters, which have been written as one paragraph. Decide where you think new paragraphs should be started and rewrite each letter accordingly, retaining the original layout.

a)

Dear Ms Ho

I have pleasure in enclosing a cheque for £325.00. This represents the amount due to you for the work you did for us during the week beginning 26 May. I would like to raise the possibility of your doing further work for us in the month of July. At present, we are not sure of the dates during which we would require your services, but I would like to check your availability in general terms now. I would appreciate your letting me know whether you could fit in some work for us around this time. Please let me know as soon as you can. I look forward to hearing from you.

Yours sincerely

Jill Paxton

Jill Paxton (Company Secretary)

b)

Dear Mr Hampton,

I am writing to protest about the treatment of veal calves at our local port, which is in the constituency you represent. I want to make it clear that I am not a rabid animal rights protester, but merely a concerned citizen who is appalled at the cruel treatment these defenceless animals receive. To transport these animals by sea to the continent where they endure a long period of imprisonment confined in small crates is not acceptable. I hope you are making representations to the firms who profit from this trade. I have read some of your speeches about animal rights and I am sure that you are as concerned as I am about this continuing cruelty. I felt I wanted to voice my concern directly to you, so that you know that some of your constituents are very worried by this issue. I would appreciate a response to my letter.

Yours sincerely,

Valerie Long

WRITING NOTES AND MEMOS

Letter writing is not always the most appropriate form of written communication.

For example, on occasions you may want to leave a brief, informal message for a relative or friend to inform them about some change in your plans or something similar:

> Mike
> Sorry you weren't in when I called.
> Just to let you know there's a party at ken's tomorrow night. Everyone's invited. Fancy it? Bring a bottle. should be good fun. I'll call in for you round eight. Cheers.
>   Bert

> Mum and Dad
> I'm off out to a film with Carol. Have had something to eat and left yours in oven. Won't be late, I promise, but please don't wait up for me.
>   Meg.

These are informal notes. The tone and language are appropriate for their context and purpose.

Note, for example, the use of incomplete or **minor** sentences:

Should be good fun.   Cheers.   Won't be late.

Managing your time is an important part of everyday life and when you are very busy it is often useful to write yourself a memory aid or memorandum (memo for short).

At work, senior colleagues will often give you various tasks to accomplish. It is important to negotiate with each of them a time by which each of these tasks has to be completed. You have to be realistic about how long each task will take and the number of tasks you can reasonably take on. Then make a list of priorities of this kind:

1 Type MD's letters by 5p.m.
2 Phone Hood and Co. about delivery dates
3 Write exploratory letter to new suppliers about packaging materials
4 Gather suggestions for agenda of monthly meeting
5 Find out statistics on ownership of VCRs
6 Inform Heads of Departments about change of date of July meeting
7 Order new requisition forms
8 Contact Philip Dunne about meeting

These brief notes will be enough to remind you of the jobs you have to do. They may overlap with one another, but it is also useful to have an order of priority in mind, which is reflected in the list you write.

MEMOS AT WORK

At work, you will frequently have to write 'notes' or memos to colleagues.

Jean: Just a short note to ask you to remind me tomorrow to write a memo to Jim about writing a memo to the boss about last week's memo from sales.

These memos vary in their degree of formality, just like letters. How formal or informal they are in tone and language depends on their purpose, how well the writer knows the receiver and how widely they will be circulated and read.

For example, here are some office memos in ascending order of formality:

1

M E M O R A N D U M

From: David   **Date:** 14 July 2004

To: May

Re: Departmental meeting

Are we going to raise the issue of the annual budget on Thursday? I'm not sure whether it is right to do so at this meeting or not. Any thoughts? Get back to me if you have. I'm in the office tomorrow afternoon if you want a quick chat. How was your break?

David .

This memo is between colleagues who are on first name terms with one another and clearly are friends as well as colleagues. Therefore, the tone is quite informal, but businesslike. The memo is not meant to be circulated to anyone else, especially as the last sentence asks a 'personal' question.

The tone of memo **2** opposite is businesslike, but there are 'personal touches' to it as well: the writer adds his first name at the end and there is a reference to requisition forms that have 'gone missing'. It is more formal than the first example above, because the memo has a wider circulation than merely between two friendly colleagues.

2

MEMORANDUM

From: Jim Taylor   Date: 18 March 2004
        Supplies

To: All Department Heads

Re: Annual requisitions

I want to remind all departmental heads that annual requisitions
must be with me by 25 March. Please avoid the situation we were
in last year. Any problems, please contact me. However,
colleagues should be aware there is a month's delay in delivery
times at present. If your supply of requisition forms has dried up
or 'gone missing', I have replacements.

3

This is a formal
memorandum from the
managing director of a
company to all
employees. It includes
sending them best wishes
for 'the festive season',
but it is still formal in
tone, because of the
relationship of the writer
to the recipients.

• • • • • • • MEMORANDUM • • • • • • •

From: Jean Malone   **Date**: 18 December 1998

To: All staff

As we approach the festive season holiday period, I would
like to thank all employees for their efforts during the past
year. These efforts have seen production levels reach new
peaks. Our company faces 1999 with every confidence;
indeed, as we face up to the next millennium, we can
congratulate ourselves on our past performance.

However, the world out there is highly competitive
and we cannot afford to rest on our laurels.

Prospects for continued employment look very good,
but that, of course, depends on our continuing efforts to
make this firm profitable.

I would like to wish you a very happy time over the
festive season and I look forward to seeing you back at
work on January 2nd.

Jean Malone

Managing Director

✓ Checkpoint B

Read each of the following notes or memos. Firstly, decide which of the following descriptions is most appropriate for the tone and language used in each: very informal, informal, quite formal, formal. Then, write down a brief description of the relationship of the writer to the receiver(s) and the purpose of the note or memo.

a)

Hi, Tracey.

Was passing and thought I'd pop in to see you. Sorry you were out at lunch. How about a film on Saturday? There's the new Tom Cruise on at the Odeon. Give me a ring. Have lots of news.

karen.

b)

Memo: from Principal to all teachers

Date: 2 February 2006

Re: end-of-term exam papers

May I remind teachers that all exam papers must be marked by the 16th of this month. I would like to emphasise the importance of checking the addition of marks, as last year there were some serious errors. Mark lists must be with the relevant HOD by the 16th as well. Students must not be informed of their results until the papers have been checked by the HOD. Please keep to this way of doing things.

Norman Walker

Principal

c)

To Alistair   Thursday 4.30p.m.

Sorry I missed you today. As you know, I will be out of the office until Wednesday next. I have left you a proposal to prepare for the board meeting. It is really important we get it ready on time. A lot hangs on its acceptance. So do your best. There are some details that have to be checked - hope I've indicated where clearly. You can always contact me on voicemail if there is a problem.

Valerie.

SENDING FAXES AND E-MAILS

Most businesses use fax or e-mail for high-speed communication of written messages and documents.

A **fax** can be sent from a fax machine or via a computer; both use a telephone link to transmit a written communication and/or an image.

The first page of a fax in formal business communications is what is called a 'fax cover sheet'.

It gives essential information:

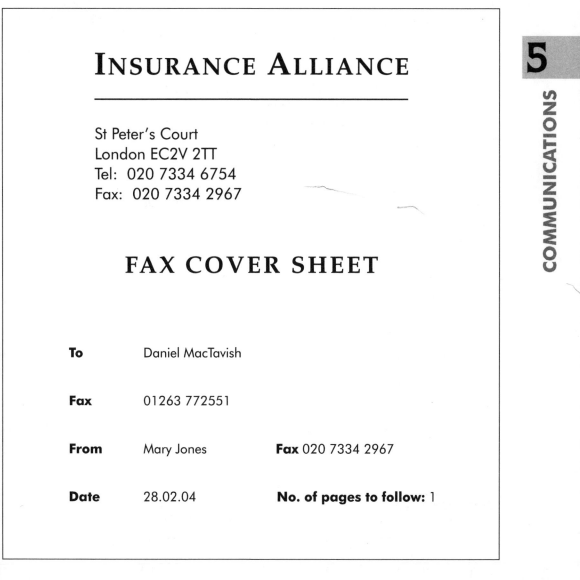

INSURANCE ALLIANCE

St Peter's Court
London EC2V 2TT
Tel: 020 7334 6754
Fax: 020 7334 2967

FAX COVER SHEET

To   Daniel MacTavish

Fax   01263 772551

From   Mary Jones   **Fax** 020 7334 2967

Date   28.02.04   **No. of pages to follow:** 1

After this fax cover sheet, there will follow the page(s) of the communication itself.

It is usual for large organisations to have separate telephone and fax numbers. Smaller organisations are likely to have a combined telephone and fax machine.

An **e-mail** is now the most common form of text communication within and between business organisations. The message can be typed directly into a document within the e-mail program on the computer, and 'sent' without any printed copy being necessary. Files containing additional documents and images can be 'attached' to an e-mail and then opened by the receiver. E-mails are more efficient and quicker than faxes and, unlike faxes, can be sent to a large number of people at once. However, if you want to send someone a copy of a document that is not already available in electronic form, then in order to e-mail it your computer has to have the ability to scan the document, whereas a fax machine scans it automatically as part of the faxing process.

E-mails have the convenient advantage that they automatically identify the sender, date and time of each message, so there is no need for a formal 'cover sheet'. The receiver can also reply very easily by typing a response into the same document and sending it back. Because of this immediacy, and because they are sent so frequently and so quickly, e-mails are often written in a more informal, casual style than letters and faxes. However, it is still important to bear in mind who is likely to be reading your e-mail, and to write it appropriately.

Have a look at the following example of an e-mail message and response sent between two business colleagues:

```
wafflebook cover - urgent!                   Fri, 17. Sept 2004  11:54 AM

To:  h.murphy@johnjones.co.uk
Subject:  wafflebook cover - urgent!
_____

Harriet
Really like it but NB Pete's name is misspelt on the cover - it's Waffle
not Woffle.
Best wishes
Sally

----- Original Message -----
From: "Harriet" <h.murphy@johnjones.co.uk>
To: "Sally" <salkelly@hotmail.com>; "Pete" <peterwaffle@bookspell.co.uk>
Sent: Thursday, September 16, 2004 9:32 AM
Subject: FW: Business and communication

Dear Sally and Pete
Please find attached the cover for your book, which we plan to put into
our new catalogue. We need you to respond on this pretty quickly, please!!
Thanks
Harriet
```

Activities 3–6

3 Write three short messages using contrasting degrees of formality:

a) an e-mail to a friend telling him/her about your recent holiday

b) a letter to an ex-teacher asking whether he or she can provide a reference for you

c) a fax to a newspaper's letter column in which you put forward your views about a current issue.

4 Think about some things you have been meaning to do in your life. Write yourself a memo in the form of a list of things to do in order of priority.

5 If you are in employment now, make a list of tasks you have to carry out in the near future in order of priority. If you are not in employment at present, imagine yourself in a job situation you would like to be in. Make a list of possible tasks connected with this job in order of priority.

6 Write notes or memos in the appropriate tone and language for each of the following contexts:

a) your parents are returning from holiday, but you have decided to go out for the evening. You have done your best to prepare a welcome for them in your absence.

b) your boss at work has been away from the workplace for most of the day. You have taken several phone calls for him or her, but you have had to leave work early for a dental appointment. You write a memo summarising the information.

c) you are the department head in a small company. You have to remind the staff in your department that they have to submit their claims for expenses (travelling, hospitality) by a certain date. You circulate an appropriate memo.

SKILLCHECK Check these statements to assess what you have learnt from this chapter. If you cannot honestly tick all of these statements, then go back over the relevant section.

❏ I understand the difference between Standard English and informal English and realise that the use of Standard English is appropriate in formal pieces of writing.

❏ I accept that there are degrees of formality in writing and that it is important to choose the appropriate level of formality (register) for a particular purpose.

❏ I realise that the layout of letters varies according to their purpose and context.

❏ I appreciate the need for clear paragraphing in more formal letters.

❏ I appreciate the need to manage time and organise things that must be done in the form of a list.

❏ I understand the purpose of memorandums and the different levels of formality in their language according to their purposes.

6

NOTE TAKING, SUMMARISING, REPORT WRITING

- **If you are a student, there will be numerous occasions when you will have to make notes based on what you are reading.**
- **In the workplace, there may be times when you are asked to make a summary of the contents of a document.**
- **The ability to take notes in this way as a memory aid saves you time and energy and is a useful skill.**

SKIMMING AND SCANNING

Skimming is when you quickly glance at a document or a book in order to get a general view of the contents.

For example, if you were skimming this book, you might read the contents page and flick through the chapter headings to get an idea of what topics the book deals with.

Some books have an **index** which lists the topics dealt with in alphabetical order with page references.

Once you have the information you want from the contents page or index, you may turn to particular pages and let your eye skim over the text. The object is not to read every word, but to get a quick impression of what the text is communicating.

Scanning is when you scan the pages of a document or book because you are 'hunting' for something in particular.

Scanning is different in that you know what you are looking for in a book. You want information on a particular topic, so once again you will scan the contents page and index (if there is one) to find the relevant section(s) of the book. Scanning involves focusing on what you want to find.

HIGHLIGHTING AND GIVING EMPHASIS TO TEXT

Highlighting, underlining and using bold type are some of the ways of reminding yourself, or someone else, of the most essential points that a piece of writing contains.

Highlighting consists of marking particularly relevant sections of written information with a coloured marker pen. It is more than just underlining, because the relevant section is highlighted by the use of the coloured pen and the text can still be read through the highlighting.

Consider this letter, for example, and note how particular sentences have been highlighted:

Dear Ms Bristow

Thank you for your recent letter. The information you request will be circulated at the end of the month. This is the earliest date possible, given the very tight schedule.

Meanwhile, however, I would very much appreciate your sending me back the information sheet suitably filled in by the end of this week. Until I have this information, I cannot complete the information booklet.

I trust this answers your query. If you require any further information, please phone Edwin Stride, our publications manager.

Your sincerely

Gina Norman

Gina Norman
Research and Development Manager

Note how certain essential information in the letter has been highlighted.

This will act as a memory aid to the 'receiver' or addressee.

Alternatively, perhaps someone else (a secretary, for example) has highlighted the sections for the addressee to draw her attention to the essential information it contains.

At work, part of your duties is to open and read your boss's letters, then highlight the most important information the letters contain and put them on her/his desk. Read the following letters and decide which sections you would highlight for your boss's attention.

a)

Dear Mr Smith

The books that you ordered should be delivered by the 30th of this month. Unfortunately, there has been a problem at our usual printers and the reprinting of some titles has been delayed.

However, I should also inform you that we normally ask customers to send in orders at least a month before delivery is required.

I also enclose a list of deleted titles that will no longer be available. If you have any queries, please contact our sales department on 01453 764328, ext 21.

Yours sincerely

Geoff Langton

Geoff Langton
Sales Manager

b)

Dear Ms Clough

I am sorry that you were dissatisfied with your recent stay at The Imperial, Linden. We consider the Imperial to be the flagship hotel of our group and we are concerned that you had so many complaints about standards and service.

I have personally contacted the Imperial manager to discuss the details of your complaints. On his behalf, I apologise for the inadequacies of the dinner. He did stress, however, that it is preferable to raise these matters at the time. As far as the other complaints are concerned, we are, at present, refurbishing the hotel and standards are accordingly not as high as we would like them to be.

In the circumstances, we would like to offer you, as compensation, two nights free accommodation with dinner included at the Imperial or any other hotel in the group. This offer is open until the end of May next year.

I hope you find this satisfactory and that we can look forward to your being our guest again in the near future.

Yours sincerely

Claire Michie

Claire Michie
Group Manager

TAKING NOTES AND WRITING SUMMARIES

Taking notes is a skill that is useful in all kinds of contexts.

In your studies, there will be times when you need to make brief notes to remind you about something important you have read.

In addition, you might be asked to make notes from written information with a view to your writing a summary of the important points that someone else can use.

When you are making notes on something you are reading:

* Keep your notes brief.

   It is best to note only **key words**, **definitions** or **explanations**, and some **headings** or **sub-headings**.

   The most common fault in note taking is to write too much. Do not copy down whole paragraphs or even sentences.

* Organise the notes so you can easily make sense of them at a later date.

   Number the essential points. Underline key words. Use a highlighter pen to draw attention to particular things.

As an illustration, imagine you have had to read Shakespeare's play 'Hamlet' and want to make very brief notes on its plot. Your notes might look something like these:

1 *Hamlet's psychological troubles*
2 *his attitude to his mother's marriage*
3 *the question of the succession to throne*
4 *Hamlet's reasons for not killing uncle – fear of unknown, while at prayer*
5 *is Hamlet just excusing himself for delay? Real reasons?*
6 *possibly no one explanation. Does he think too much?*

These notes are brief but concise, clear and numbered. They could be the basis for later revision, or for a short summary of the original piece of writing.

When you are reading a document of some kind in order to summarise the contents, follow this process:

- select the essential points from each section of the document by underlining and numbering them
- ignore any repetition or lists
- use important names or technical terms from the original
- write concise notes in brief sentences
- check these against the document to make sure you have included all the essential points
- write the summary, making it a continuous and concise piece of writing that uses paragraphing appropriately.

Imagine that at work you have been asked to read the following passage and make a summary of the main points.

THE RISE OF THE PC

The market in the United Kingdom for the sale of personal computers will continue to expand, especially as we now live in the age of internet and cyberspace. About 42 per cent of households own a PC, which is a substantially higher percentage than in Germany, Italy, France, Sweden, Holland, Belgium or Spain. The percentage of British households with children that have personal computers is even higher: 59 per cent.

The fact is that people perceive the latest computer to be a status symbol second only to a car. However, differences in how they are used emerge as being linked to social class: most middle-class parents see PCs as educational tools, whereas, in most working-class households, a PC is seen as a source of entertainment.

There is a distinct gender difference as well. Computers are predominantly a male obsession. The vast majority of computer games, for example, are aimed at the male half of the population.

Computer literacy is essential in finding well-paid employment in an increasingly technological age. If women and the less well-off in society are not skilled in using computers, this will be a handicap in the workplace as more and more firms rely on computer-based networks.

Your first reading of the passage will involve underlining and numbering key points. As a result, the passage might look like this:

THE RISE OF THE PC

The <u>market in the United Kingdom</u> for the sale of <u>personal computers</u> will continue to <u>expand</u> (1), especially as we now live in the age of <u>internet and cyberspace</u> (2). <u>About 42 per cent of households</u> (3) own a PC, which is a substantially <u>higher percentage than in Germany, Italy, France, Sweden, Holland, Belgium or Spain</u> (4). The percentage of British <u>households with children</u> that have personal computers is even higher: <u>59 per cent</u> (5).

The fact is that people perceive the latest computer to be a <u>status symbol</u> (6) second only to a car. However, differences in how they are used emerge as being linked to <u>social class</u>: most <u>middle-class parents</u> see PCs as <u>educational tools</u>, whereas, in most <u>working-class households</u>, a PC is seen as a <u>source of entertainment</u>. (7)

There is a distinct <u>gender difference</u> as well. Computers are predominantly <u>a male obsession</u>. The vast majority of computer games, for example, are aimed at the male half of the population.

<u>Computer literacy</u> is essential in <u>finding well-paid employment</u> (8) in an increasingly technological age. If <u>women and the less well-off</u> in society are <u>not skilled</u> in using computers, this will be a <u>handicap in the workplace</u> (9) as more and more firms rely on computer-based networks.

The next step is to write concise notes in brief sentences:

The UK market in PCs will expand in the internet and cyberspace age.

42 per cent of British households have PCs, more than in most other European countries.

This figure is higher for households with children.

PCs are status symbols.

Class differences emerge: middle-class parents see a PC as education tool, working-class households use them for entertainment.

Gender differences show computers are male obsession.

Employment prospects improve with level of computer literacy.

Women and less well-off in society will be at a disadvantage in the job market.

These sentences become the basis for a continuous piece of writing that is a summary of the key points of the passage:

THE RISE OF THE PC

The UK market in personal computers, in the age of internet and cyberspace, will expand. At present, 42 per cent of households possess one, a far larger percentage than in most other European countries. This percentage is higher for households with children.

The PC is seen as a status symbol, although most middle-class parents use it as an educational tool, whilst working-class households employ it as a source of entertainment. Men are obsessed with computers. As computer literacy is essential in the job market, a lack of computing skills will put women and the less well-off at a disadvantage.

NOTES, SUMMARIES AND REPORTS

Using less than half of the words in the original passage, this summary includes all the key points required. It is concisely written and reads like a continuous piece of writing.

Activity 1

At work, you have been asked to make a concise summary of the following passage, including only the key points. Follow the various stages outlined above before writing the completed version of your summary.

The issue of working as a team was discussed at length. Several employees said they would welcome a course designed to help everyone work as a unit. An external adviser could be employed to help departments work more closely together. Some speakers said that much more could be achieved if staff knew what other people were involved with and what they were thinking.

Other colleagues opposed the idea that advice was needed about working as a team, saying that they worked well together already. Some were against bringing in an outsider and thought that if a team-building course were run, then someone from inside the firm could organise it. A few staff were worried about the expense involved in setting up such a course.

Despite the different opinions, it was generally thought that the issue of teamwork was central to the success of the business. Many stated that not enough information filtered down from the top to the lower levels. There was too much of a 'them' and 'us' attitude from the managers. It was decided to discuss this issue at the next meeting.

REPORT WRITING

At work, you may be asked at some stage to write a report. This could be of a meeting, conference, a training course or something similar, or it could be of a particular initiative, work practice, document or new work procedure.

Whatever it is, the report will have to be precise, clear and ordered, if it is to communicate effectively to the 'consumers' of the report. The effectiveness of the communication depends on clarity of language and organisation.

The objectives of the report need to be spelt out. This can be done in a main heading:

Report of One-Day Conference on Staff Training, Universal Hall, Barchester on 26th May 2005.

Or it can be stated under the sub-heading 'Content' or 'Subject':

Subject: report of one-day conference on staff training held at Universal Hall, Barchester, 26th May, 2005

Headings and sub-headings are very useful means of ordering the content of a report and breaking it up into manageable sections for your readers. The use of **bold type**, *italic type* and <u>underlining</u> can also be very helpful:

Aims of Conference

The delegates were asked to consider how staff training could be improved and how limited resources could be used to train as many staff as possible within a relatively short period of time.

Conference programme
Delegates were addressed by the company's <u>Head of Training, Joy Castle</u>. Ms Castle stated that it was the aim of the training department to have **all staff** involved in at least **one one-day training course per year**.

The above extract from a report starts with a main heading: **Aims of Conference**. After the first paragraph, there are a number of sub-headings that are printed in italic. Variations in type-face, print styles and size of type are useful means of drawing attention to different aspects of the report.

Note, too, that certain details are underlined and others are emphasised with bold type.

Other likely sub-headings that a report like this might use are:

Objectives	*Proposals*
Summary of discussion	*Conclusions*
Conference resolutions	*Comments*

The aim should be to produce a concise and clear report for any interested individuals who were not present at the event. The more 'signposts' you, the writer of the report, provide for your readers, the more effective the communication.

Activities 2 and 3

2 Choose any book that is likely to contain information about a particular topic in which you are interested. Firstly, **skim** through the book to get a clear idea of what the book is about. Write a paragraph summarising the contents.

   Secondly, decide which aspect of the overall subject of the book you are particularly interested in. Use the contents page and the index (if there is one) to find the relevant section(s) or page(s). Then **scan** these and find the information you want.

3 Write a report on any 'event' that you have recently attended. It could be a meeting of some kind (a conference, a fan or supporters' club, for example) or some public demonstration about which you have been asked to write a formal report. You may imagine such a meeting or demonstration, if you prefer. Your 'brief' is to write a concise, clear report of the event for someone in authority over you, who was not present. You must use main headings, sub-headings, and devices such as underlining and bold type (if you are typing or using a word-processor).

6

NOTES, SUMMARIES AND REPORTS

6

NOTES, SUMMARIES AND REPORTS

7
AGENDAS AND MINUTES

■ **Formal meetings usually have a written agenda, which is a list of business items due to be dealt with during the meeting.**

■ **Agendas are usually circulated before a meeting to all those due to attend. This enables participants to prepare for the meeting by thinking about the issues to be raised, researching relevant facts and figures and discussing issues with colleagues.**

DRAWING UP AN AGENDA

Agendas may vary in their format, but they generally follow a set pattern.

- **Apologies for any absence** (Those not able to attend the meeting send their apologies and reasons for absence via someone in attendance.)
- **The reading of the minutes of the previous meeting** (A record of the previous meeting has been kept in the form of **minutes**; these are read, usually by the secretary, and it has to be agreed by those present that they are an accurate record.)
- **Matters arising from the minutes** (Participants may raise points relating to the minutes, perhaps asking what has happened about a certain matter since the previous meeting.)
- **Correspondence** (The secretary reports to the meeting about any letters that have been received and their contents.)
- **Secretary's report** (If the organisation has a secretary, he or she gives a report on anything relevant that has occurred since the previous meeting.)
- **Treasurer's report** (The treasurer reports on financial matters.)
- **Items of business** (The main items to be dealt with in the meeting.)
- **Any other business** (Participants can raise matters that have not been listed under items of business.)
- **Date of next meeting** (The participants agree the date of the next meeting.)

Agendas for meetings at a workplace may well vary from this format. For example, it may not be necessary to have a secretary's and a treasurer's report, unless the meeting is connected with a social club, a trade union, professional association, or similar organisation.

The important thing for you to remember is that most formal meetings are preceded by the circulation of an agenda and this agenda will be created according to a certain formula.

Consider this agenda for the monthly meeting of the social club committee at an engineering works:

HARPER AND LOW
ENGINEERING WORKS
SOCIAL CLUB COMMITTEE

The next meeting of the social club committee will take place on 29 March at 5p.m. in the Green Room.

Agenda

1 Apologies for absence
2 Minutes of previous meeting
3 Correspondence
4 Secretary's report
5 Treasurer's report
6 Annual outing
7 Date of annual dance
8 Employment of cleaners
9 Any other business
10 Date of next meeting

At work, you may well attend meetings where agendas have been circulated previously, or be asked to write an agenda based on instructions given to you.

You should make yourself familiar with the format and vocabulary used in agendas in order for you to participate in meetings and prepare agendas in advance.

KEEPING MINUTES

Minutes are the formal records of meetings held. They are strict and objective records of what happened and of what was decided at a meeting. There is no place for personal opinions in minutes. The person writing the minutes has to be as objective and accurate in recording the minutes as possible.

Minutes should consist of:

- A note of when and where the meeting took place
- Where it is appropriate, a list of the people present and a note of apologies received (if there were too many people present to list individually, the numbers attending should be recorded)
- The minutes of the previous meeting (any amendments to the minutes are recorded and the fact that they were agreed as an accurate record by the meeting is noted)
- Matters arising (a summary of any discussion arising from the minutes of the previous meeting)
- Correspondence (a summary of letters received and replies sent)
- Secretary's and Treasurer's reports: a summary of the reports
- Items of business (usually the main part of the minutes consisting of a summary of points raised and decisions reached)
- Any other business (a summary of matters raised under 'AOB')
- Date of next meeting (the date and time of the next meeting is given).

Consider the sample minutes on page 92. They are the minutes of the Harper and Low social club committee meeting. The agenda for this meeting is on page 90.

AGENDAS AND MINUTES

Minutes of Harper and Low Engineering Works Social Club Committee held on the 29 March at 5p.m. in the Green Room of the Social Club.

Members present
June Ogilvy (chairperson), Len Murray (secretary), Mabel Green (treasurer), Frank Little, Joy Goulding, Karen Oliver

Apologies for absence
These were received from Mrs Reid and Mr Wilson.

Minutes of previous meeting
The minutes of the meeting of 26 February last were read and agreed as an accurate record.

Correspondence
The secretary read the contents of a letter received from the social club committee of Henderson's. The chairperson suggested that the Henderson's committee should be contacted and suggestions for joint social activities made.

Secretary's report
The secretary reported that membership was increasing, but that new employees had to be encouraged to join.

Treasurer's report
Annual subscriptions were now overdue; treasurer made suggestion that subscriptions should be increased next year.

Annual outing
The annual works outing was discussed but no final decision was made. Suggestions included a visit to a theme park, a day in London and a day trip to France.

Date of annual dance
The date was fixed for 17 June.

Employment of cleaners
Concern was expressed about the cleanliness of the social club premises. It was decided to investigate the possibility of regular employment of cleaners.

Any other business
None.

Date of next meeting
The next meeting will be on 30 April in the Green Room at 5p.m.

Anyone reading these minutes will get a clear idea of what was discussed and decided at the meeting. The minutes also stand as a formal record of what took place at the meeting, in case some dispute about a decision, or some other matter, arises later.

Activities 1 and 2

1 Write agendas for any of the following meetings, following the format described above:

a) Your school or college students' association is due to hold its annual meeting to discuss any relevant matters.

b) The committee of a social club or society you belong to is due to hold its monthly meeting.

c) Your head of department at work asks you to prepare an agenda for the regular departmental meeting based on her/his instructions.

2 You have attended one or both of the following meetings and you have been asked to write the minutes. Be accurate, precise and clear.

a) You attend the committee meeting of a society devoted to a special interest (a youth organisation, a charity, a sports club) and later write the minutes of the meeting.

b) You have been asked to write the minutes of a monthly meeting of the department of the firm in which you are employed.

SKILLCHECK Check these statements to assess what you have learnt from this chapter. If you cannot honestly tick all of these statements, then go back over the relevant section.

❏ I understand how an agenda is put together and the kind of format it follows.

❏ I know what minutes are and how they should be written.

7

AGENDAS AND MINUTES

8

APPLYING
FOR JOBS

■ If you are looking for employment, it is very probable that you will have to write a letter or fill in an application form.

■ Some applicants for jobs are judged by a personal interview only, but, increasingly, those seeking employment have to present themselves in a favourable light through the written word.

   This may take various forms:

   • an initial letter of application written as a general enquiry rather than as a reply to a specific advertisement

   • a letter in response to an advertisement that has asked for applications in writing

   • a curriculum vitae (CV) which is a summary of personal information, educational qualifications and employment experience usually enclosed with a letter of application

   • the filling-in of an application form.

■ Whatever the form your application for a job takes, remember that a written application must say something significant about you. It represents all that a prospective employer will know about you. It is up to you to make a good impression through this written document. After all, if an employer receives a number of applications for a post, applicants will be summoned to an interview or rejected on the basis of the impression the written application makes on the reader(s).

A GENERAL LETTER OF ENQUIRY

Sometimes when you are looking for a job, it is a matter of letting employers know that you are out there looking. Often, you will be responding to specific job advertisements; at other times, you may have to take the initiative and write directly to a firm or organisation that you think might be able to use your skills.

Remember, if you write a general letter of application like this, your prospective employer will only have your letter to judge you by. Therefore, you must present yourself in the best possible light.

Consider these contrasting examples of a general letter of enquiry sent to the same firm by different applicants.

17 Greenland Avenue

Barstow

12 July 2005

Dear Sir,

I have just left college and am looking for a job. I was wondering whether you had anything for me. I have several exam passes and am interested in working for your firm. I have some work experience through college. I would like to come and see you some time. I hope to hear from you.

Yours sincerely,

24 Roman Road
Barstow
BW1 4RT

12 July 2003

Personnel Director
Dean Postcard Company
Unit 48
Barstow Industrial Estate
Barstow BW3 4GH

Dear Sir/Madam

I am writing to enquire whether you have any job vacancies at your firm for which I could be considered. I have just left Barstow College and am looking for work.

I have several passes at GCSE, including English, Maths, History, Business Studies and French. I have had some work experience arranged through college and I can supply further details of that, if required. My college tutors can provide you with references.

My main interest would be to work in the office of your firm, starting with general office duties. I have experience of word-processing and am fairly skilled in using computers. Alternatively, I would consider a job in the sales and dispatch departments.

This is a preliminary letter to let you know that I would like a job with your firm. I can supply much more detailed information on request and I am available for interview at any time. I have lived all my life in Barstow and intend to stay here and find employment.

I hope this letter is of interest to you. I look forward to hearing from you.

Yours faithfully

Deborah King

Deborah King

REPLYING TO JOB ADVERTISEMENTS

Very often you will see an advertisement in a newspaper or magazine, or in some other location, for a particular job, for which you have to apply in writing. Sometimes these advertisements mention that you should include a curriculum vitae or CV; sometimes the advertisement mentions 'career information'.

Whether it is mentioned in the advertisement or not, it is generally a good idea to include a CV with a letter unless the employer specifies that an application form should be used.

SECURE INSURANCE SERVICES LTD
Our company is expanding and we are looking to recruit

TRAINEE SALES PERSONNEL

Experience in the insurance industry is not required. If you have some GCSE passes under your belt, are keen and of a personable appearance, are aged between 18 and 25, we would like to hear from you.

We can offer:

- a full training programme
- promotion prospects
- a satisfactory starting salary while training
- a company car and pension scheme

If you would like a challenge and are determined to succeed, please write with full details to:
Derek Hill, Secure Insurance Services, Greenhill GW1 3UG

8

APPLYING FOR JOBS

This advertisement requires a reply that will consist of two parts: a letter and a CV. The CV will list the details of your educational qualifications and job experience, if relevant.

Always respond to a job advertisement in the specific ways that the advertisement lists. If the advertisement mentions qualifications, special skills and/or experience, then make sure you deal with these points in your application. The accurate reading of job advertisements is an important part of responding to them.

Once again, if the advertising firm are to show any further interest in you, you have to present yourself in as favourable a light as possible. Therefore, it is worthwhile spending some time in getting the letter and CV right.

---

26 Monastery Gardens
Beeton SR1 6NL

9 August 2004

Derek Hill
Secure Insurance Services
Greenhill GW1 3UG

Dear Mr Hill

I am replying to your advertisement for trainee sales personnel in the 'Daily News' of 3 August.

I have had some experience of sales work, although that was not in the insurance industry. I am at present unemployed, because the firm I had been working for went out of business. I can, however, supply relevant references on request. I think I have already proved that I have some talent for work in sales and I certainly like a challenge in my work.

I enclose a full CV as requested. I will be available for interview at any time.

I hope my application is of interest to you. If I can supply any further information, please contact me at the above address. I look forward to hearing from you.

Yours sincerely

Ali Shiraz

Ali Shiraz

This letter gives enough detail to introduce the writer to the addressee, but leaves the main detail for the CV that has been requested. The tone is 'keen' without overdoing it; the presentation is immaculate; the content is business-like but not 'over-formal'.

WRITING A CV

Your CV is a kind of summary of your personal details, educational qualifications and job experience. It must be clearly presented and accurate in detail.

Consider this example:

Name	Ali Shiraz
Address	26 Monastery Gardens, Beeton, East Swickton SR1 6NL
Telephone	01345 668523
Date of Birth	29.2.87

Education	1991–1997 Beeton Junior School
	1997–2003 East Swickton College
	GCSE subjects: English, Maths,
	                      Business Studies
	                      History, French, Drama

Employment Experience	2004–2005 Sales Assistant, Bannington's
	           North Street, Beeton.
	2003–2004 Assistant storesperson, Hegley Bros,
	           Beeton
	2002–2003 Hairdresser's assistant (part-time),
	           Hairwego, Beeton

General Information	Have experience in using word processors and computers Fluent in French Interests: drama, cinema, skiing
Referees	L. Hutton (General Manager), Bannington's, North Street, Bannington. Y. Murray, 'Hairwego', 16 Cheapside, Beeton.

There are several things to note about the presentation and content of this CV:

- it is clearly and neatly presented with adequate spacing to enable a reader to take in the information
- under 'Employment Experience' the applicant's previous jobs are listed starting with the most recent one and working backwards in time

- some general information has been included: special skills and interests
- two referees have been given: these individuals should be approached for their permission to be named before you refer to them in any application. Clearly, it is also important to use referees who will give you a satisfactory reference.

Here is another job advertisement:

Junior Typist Clerk

We are searching for an intelligent, keen young man or woman, aged approximately 18–19 years, to join our financial department.

You must be able to type at speed and accurately, be computer-literate, and proficient in the use of word processors. In addition, a suitable qualification in maths would be a decided advantage.

Apply in writing, giving details of your exam qualifications, special skills and work experience, to:

Phyllis Dixon, Finance Department,
Western Media, Apollo House,
Blackstock BL1 6RY.

This advertisement is quite specific about what the company is looking for in terms of qualifications and skills. A careful reader of the advertisement might underline these words:

type at speed   computer-literate   word processors
qualification in maths   exam qualifications   special skills
work experience

Each one of these points would have to be responded to in your letter of application. Here is a sample reply:

16 Mountview Road
Blackstock BL2 3FG
4 March 2004

Phyllis Dixon
Finance Department
Western Media
Apollo House
Blackstock BL1 6RY

Dear Ms Dixon

I am writing in response to the advertisement for a junior typist clerk in the last issue of the 'Echo'.

I am eighteen years of age and I left Blackstock College last June. Since then I have been employed as a junior clerk by the Omega Insurance Company branch office in the High Street.

I have six passes at GCSE level: English, Maths, French, History, Business Studies and Theatre Studies. I type at an average speed of 40 wpm and my work has been commended for its speed and accuracy by my present employers. I have also been using an Apple computer in my job and consider myself computer-literate. I can certainly use a word processor.

Much of my work with Omega has been in accounting, so I am used to dealing with figures. I gained a Grade B pass in Maths at GCSE. I would welcome an opportunity to develop my knowledge of financial matters, if I were appointed.

I am available for interview at any time. I have informed my present employers that I am seeking a post elsewhere and they have agreed to supply me with references. Please contact T. Entwhistle, Accounts Department, Omega Insurance Company, 60 High Street, Blackstock BL1 4ED.

I count myself as both intelligent and keen and I would welcome the opportunity to work for Western Media. I hope my application is of interest and I look forward to hearing from you.

Yours sincerely

Martin Glass

Martin Glass

FILLING IN A JOB APPLICATION FORM

For some job vacancies you have to fill in a printed application form. These come in many different formats, but they must be completed with care. Once again, this will be how an employer will judge you initially. If you are to be called for an interview, you must impress the advertiser with:

- the neatness and clarity of your application
- the accuracy with which you have filled in the details
- the relevance of the detail you have supplied
- your suitability for the job
- the enthusiasm you show for the post. There may be an opportunity to display this in the form (for example, if you are asked to write something about yourself and why you are suitable for the post).

Consider this blank job application form:

E M P L O Y M E N T   A P P L I C A T I O N   F O R M   A 1 / S E

S E C T I O N **A**
Please use block letters in filling in this section of the form.

Position applied for

Full-time/part-time (delete appropriately)

Name

Address

Postcode

Home telephone number: ————————— business: —————————

Town and country of birth

Date of Birth

Section B
Education

Primary

Secondary

Further Education

Educational qualifications gained

Section C
Employment experience (list present or most recent employer first)

Section D

Write not more than 200 words about yourself including your hobbies and interests, special skills and experience, and why you think you would be suitable for the post you have applied for.

Activities 2–6

2 Look through the employment vacancies section in your local newspaper. Find a job advertisement that you think is relevant to your needs and skills. Write a letter in response to the advertisement, and prepare a CV.

3 Choose any one of the following advertisements and respond to it with a letter and CV.

Dental Receptionist Junior trainee required full-time by city centre dental practice. Apply in own writing to Box 35.

Garage mechanic required: a keen young person needed for full on-the-job training; must have working knowledge of cars and be hard-working. Applications in writing only to: The Manager, Northern Autos, 21 Green Valley, Hudson.

Trainee nurse: The Hudson Child Care Centre is looking for a caring and committed young person to train as a nurse. Applications in writing by 20 March to Mrs Janet Bonham, 34 Island Road, Garrett.

4 Respond with a letter of application to the following advertisement:

Junior Care Assistant

Residential Care Home requires a trainee care assistant. Applicants must be caring and conscientious. Apply in writing, stating educational qualifications, special skills, job experience and personal details to:

Mrs Friend, Chief Nursing Officer, Homedean Nursing Home, Homedean, HN1 5WY

5 Photocopy the application form on pages 102–104 and fill it in appropriately.

6 Scan the employment vacancies section of your local paper. Pick out jobs that you could apply for in the future that require you to send off for application forms. When you receive one, practise filling it in appropriately and neatly.

SKILLCHECK Check these statements to assess what you have learnt from this chapter. If you cannot honestly tick all of these statements, then go back over the relevant section.

❏ I have learnt how to write a general letter of enquiry about employment.

❏ I understand what a curriculum vitae is and what should be included in it.

❏ I have familiarised myself with standard job application forms and know how to fill them in appropriately.

ANSWERS to Self-assessment questionnaire

Writing in sentences

1 The level of pollution on British beaches is decreasing. This is according to a report produced by an environmental group who investigated the state of beaches up and down the country. What is a satisfactory level of pollution, however? Stating that most British beaches have improved is not saying very much. The previous situation was downright scandalous with horror stories of sewage and chemical pollution. The truth is there should be no pollution on any of our beaches. With more and more British people taking British summer holidays rather than European package tours, it is more than ever important that beaches are clean and healthy places for our kids.

2 Not a good buy because it broke when it was first used.   Always been satisfied in the past.   Asking for a refund rather than a replacement.   Because I have no confidence in the product now.   As I do appreciate the convenience of ordering goods by post.   Since I am old and cannot get to shops.   Looking forward to receiving the refund.

3 a lately I have been feeling very down
  b The woman bought the most expensive handbag in the shop
  c I got the engaged signal
  d the by-election was being dreaded
  e Do not return
  f Forget
  g The man ... appeared very friendly
  h the teacher was angry with me
  i The tournament had been a great success

Punctuation

1 It has been decided that an extra weekly practice night will take place during this month. The committee believes that, with such important games coming up, this additional commitment will be very important. Fielding practice will take priority. This has let the team down in recent matches. Every member of the first team squad is expected to turn up. If there is any difficulty about this, the individual concerned must discuss the reasons with the team captain. This decision was unanimous. We want success in the league and the cup this season. Surely we all believe that such success is within our grasp. The committee confidently expects the support of every player in this extra endeavour. Let's look forward to winning some trophies.

2 Bopper, the very successful independent record company, has just announced it has signed the new sensation of the pop world, the Pepper Pots, to a recording contract. A spokesperson for the company, Roger Maynard, said yesterday that sales of the group's discs had soared in several countries, including America, Britain, Australia, Japan and Germany. Gayle Russell, the lead singer, said she was delighted with the deal and it was especially good news on the eve of the start of the group's world tour. 'We're off to Europe tomorrow and then we take in Africa, Asia and South America. It's a long way from Bermondsey,' she added with a grin. The 'New Musical Express' reported that the group's income over the last year exceeded ten million pounds, while 'Hello' magazine is reported to have offered a huge sum for exclusive pictures of the world tour. Only 'The Guardian' and 'The Times' struck a sour note: most of their readers, they reported, have never heard of the Pots. 'They don't like us, we don't care,' retorted Jimmy Lou Harris, another member of the group.

3 Judy assumed her most sarcastic tone. 'You're not trying to tell me most designer fashion is meant to be worn,' she said. 'Most of it is just ridiculous.' 'People wear it all the time,' Melanie responded. 'They pay a lot of money for those clothes.'
'More fool them,' said Judy.
'I wish I could afford one of those designer dresses,' insisted Melanie. 'I will one day.'

'You must be crazy,' said Judy. 'You'd look silly in them.'

'You,' said Melanie, 'are just jealous.'

'Jealous!' exclaimed Judy. 'Who's jealous? Why would I be jealous? Now tell me that!'

'Because you know,' replied Melanie, 'that you wouldn't look good in really fashionable clothes.'

'What a load of baloney!' exclaimed Judy. 'Just who do you think you are?'

4 a

It's on for this evening! The restaurant's booked, the car's gearbox has been fixed and all's well with the world. I'll be home by five at the latest. My good suit's at the cleaners. It'd be great if you'd pick it up for me. The cat's food is in the cupboard. It's going to be a great evening out. I'm really looking forward to it.

Jim

b

This memo's all I'd time to leave you. It's all go this end. The deal's on. I can't see there'll be any problems. The money's settled and the dates have been agreed. I'll give you a detailed outline once the contract's with us. Congratulations all round are due. We've put a lot of effort into this. It's really great to have landed the work.

Jenny

Writing in paragraphs

Dear Sir/Madam

I am writing to enquire about the possibility of being employed in your firm as a junior office clerk.

I am sixteen years of age, have just left school and have several passes at GCSE level. These include Business Studies, English, Maths, French and Statistics. I have attended Boxley High School for the last six years.

While at school, I took part in a Job Experience scheme during which I worked in a solicitor's office. I found this work experience very interesting and rewarding. It gave me invaluable experience of office life.

I can also supply relevant references from the school and the solicitor's office where I was on Job Experience.

I am very keen to join your firm and feel confident I can fulfil any duties that would be handed to me. I am available for interview at any time.

I look forward to hearing from you in the near future.

Yours faithfully
Michelle Nichols

Spelling

Manager in Dispute with Referee

Jocky Malone, the manager of Baykop United, was involved in a violent argument with referee Joe Reid during Saturday's match at Friar Road.

After a United goal was disallowed, Malone, known as 'Jaws' in football circles, was seen to gesticulate at Reid and make menacing moves towards him. Malone had to be restrained by his colleagues.

'I wasn't aware of the incident at the time,' said the ref, 'but if I had been, I would have ordered Mr Malone from the touch-line.'

'Jaws' Malone has already been warned on several occasions, the last time for head-butting another manager. The Football League are likely to take a very gloomy view of this latest incident in the picturesque career of this controversial personality.

'I deny shouting obscenities at the ref,' said an unrepentant Malone after the match. 'I was only letting off steam. Surely I should be given the freedom to do that. I'm not a criminal after all.'

ANSWERS to
Checkpoints and Activities

PART A

Writing in sentences (page 12)

Activities 1 and 2

1

> Dear Sir
>
> In answer to your letter about my account being overdrawn, I would like to point out that my account has never been overdrawn before. This was an unfortunate oversight on my part.
>
> To avoid this situation arising again, I would like to arrange for a permanent overdraft facility. Once again, please accept my apologies. This was not intentional on my part. I will ensure, in future, that I have enough money in my account to cover any cheques that I write.
>
> I am looking forward to receiving an application form.
>
> Yours faithfully
>
> J.P. Morgan

2 The duties of the assistant storesperson include logging entries in the relevant stock book and storing in the appropriate section. In addition, the storesperson must make a record of when staff request particular equipment. The storesperson must also receive orders of supplies as they arrive from the central stores. A strict record of all such supplies must be kept. The assistant must be prepared to stand in for the senior storesperson when she or he is absent. In order to facilitate the supply of equipment, the assistant storesperson has the authority, in the absence of the senior storesperson, to sign out equipment to authorised personnel.

Activities 3 and 4
(These are sample answers only so check their structure against your sentences.)

3 a The police were completely baffled.
   b From the deep cave emerged a gigantic ant of immense proportions.
   c The circus clown amused the audience with his antics.
   d The politicians felt pleased with the campaign.
   e Interestingly, most pupils were eager to make progress.
   f The supporters behaved well for a change.
   g For the last time, the star made a concert tour.
   h In spite of everything, the holiday-makers felt satisfied with their vacation.

4 a After the kill, the birds gathered round the corpse like vultures.
   b With the result beyond doubt, the crowd were now completely shattered at the prospect of such a heavy and humiliating defeat.
   c Despite every effort, the situation became increasingly worse, much to the dismay of the aid workers.
   d The pompous newsreader introduced the important report with great solemnity.
   e After having slept for several hours and eaten a hearty breakfast, she appeared completely normal except for some external signs of her injuries.
   f The uncritical audience laughed at the movie despite its tired gags and obvious slapstick, much to the despair of the critics.
   g Because of the efforts of the defence team and the unstinting support of several MPs, justice was finally done to the men.
   h After the operation, the man actually felt worse than before, regardless of the forecasts of the surgeon.
   i Without considering the safety of the protestors and against the advice of his companions, the irate hunter fired the gun at the deer hiding in the thicket.

Activities 5–7

(Sample answers)

5 a The referee blew the final whistle and the fans erupted with joy.

b The prosecutor made a convincing case, but it was based on purely circumstantial evidence and the jury found the defendant not guilty.

c The management offered the employees a lump sum payment and advised acceptance.

d You may have your holidays in June or you can wait till August.

e The train was very late in arriving, but the guard explained the circumstances and the passengers generally accepted the apology.

6 The annual History Group outing will take place on July 27th and will be to Southend. Those wishing to book a place will have to do so by July 15th which you may do through your group leader or you may also inform Mr Greene. The total cost will be £18, which will include the cost of the hire of the coach and the cost of lunch and afternoon tea. The coach will leave from outside the building at 9.00 a.m. and return at 6.00 p.m. The History Group committee urge you to support the outing, but we need to know numbers as soon as possible.

7 Libra It is a good week for school work, but pocket money problems loom. Although visitors could cause problems, you will feel happy. Now may be the time to start new interests and you may make some new friends.
Scorpio You may face a challenge this week, so it is time for imagination and initiative. Past good deeds on your part may pay off and, at school, success may beckon or the opportunity to change courses may present itself.
Sagittarius Take care to keep up to date with things, so it could be a good time to plan your holiday. Avoid possible arguments with friends, but show resolve. School matters dominate.
Capricorn Are you working too hard or might a helping hand be available? You should be full of creative ideas, so start planning for next year. It is time to mend some past disputes.

Checkpoint B

1 a complex
b complex
c multiple
d simple
e complex
f multiple

2 a the temperature never climbed above 60°C
b The garden began to bloom in April
c I am lost in a world of my own
d the trustees feel
e you are eligible to buy another exactly the same at a reduced price

Activities 8–14

(Sample answers)

8 a As they had overslept, the parents hurriedly packed the cases, while the children got dressed.

b The film was not popular in Britain, despite the fact that it had been a huge success in America, surprising the American critics, who had given it bad reviews.

c As night began to fall, the police siren echoed across the city.

d As they had a deadline for its completion and because they were working on a bonus scheme, the workmen toiled over the extension all day, which pleased their employers.

e Because two rival dealers were present, the bidding became very fierce at the auction, which meant that it was profitable for both vendors and auctioneers.

9 a Because someone had thrown an object on the line, the train arrived late at its destination.

b You can forget that, unless something changes, as there will be no time.

c Since you want to know, she was that type of person, although she had some redeeming features.

d In spring, the garden must be renewed, although nature takes care of that for you, unless the winter has been particularly severe.

e If we are being realistic about this matter, crime statistics are notoriously misleading, because no one knows how to compile them accurately.

f Failure to comply is a serious offence, because it can cause inconvenience to others, although it can turn out to be even more serious than that.

g Because the post is an extremely responsible one, applicants must be experienced, although inexperienced individuals with flair and imagination will be considered, because the firm is determined to appoint the very best person available.

h I can offer many relevant qualifications, as I have been studying this subject at college for a number of years, because I have always wanted to succeed in this line of work.

10a The woman, who had been a last-minute applicant, gave a very impressive speech.

b The hero of the film, who was played by Sylvester Stallone, was incredibly brave.

c Laughter, which seems to be in short supply nowadays, is a great healer.

d Many contributions, some of which were extremely generous, were made.

e We, who were in at the beginning of this, are witnessing the end of an era, which, naturally, is a great sadness to us all.

f Computer technology, which was virtually unknown 25 years ago, has made great advances.

g Proceed to the loading bay, which is at the end of the road.

h Can you, who are supposed to know all the facts, give me an answer that will satisfy your critics?

11 a If you dare, mention that to him, because it would provoke a strong reaction, which would result in a lively meeting.

b Although it would appear to be a simple enough arrangement, the legal consequences are far-reaching, which should be a worry to all those who are thinking of becoming involved, because they would be held to be personally responsible.

c Because the family had requested it, the priest said the prayer, which was a simple request for forgiveness, but no one seemed offended.

d Perhaps there is room for doubt after all, which should come as no surprise to anyone who has studied the case, as it has created serious misgivings in the minds of many lawyers who have specialised in this area.

e As there have been so many applicants, the appointment will be made in two weeks' time, which will give the committee, who are anxious to make the right decision, plenty of time to consider.

f Because goods are frequently returned, you must always issue a receipt to customers, who must then produce it when they want to make an exchange or ask for a refund.

g Before the decision was taken, every option was considered and all angles investigated, which, of course, had to be done, if all the parties involved were to be satisfied, which I now think is truly the case.

h Although human existence can be very happy, into every life a little rain must fall, which is something everyone must learn and the sooner they learn it the better.

12 Each employee must attend one residential course per year, but there will be a selection to choose from. It is obligatory to choose at least one, as the management consider this an essential part of every employee's training, but special circumstances, for example, family obligations, will be taken into account. Advice is available from the training department or you may also consult your supervisor. There will be no cost to employees for the course and all travelling expenses will be refunded.

13 The world of work can be daunting for many school-leavers because, instead of a cosy school or college environment, young people are often faced with a large anonymous organisation. As this organisation may appear not to care much for the individual, the new, young employee may feel lost. Although some firms are aware of the problem and look after new employees, others dismally fail to do so.

In a situation like this, it is easy for young people to feel alienated. Because they may develop anti-work attitudes, low morale may result. An attitude of doing as little as possible may take hold, which is neither good for the young person nor productive for the employer.

Firms must have a reception policy for new employees. They must appoint experienced and sympathetic members of staff to take care of young people in particular, a policy which will pay off in the future. Because firms should want their staff to stay with them, staff loyalty has to be earned. As a happy employee is a productive employee, each member of the work-force should feel part of the organisation.

14

Dear Sir/Madam,

I am writing to complain about a pair of trousers that I bought from your mail order firm last month.

Although I wore the trousers on only a few occasions, I found that they were coming apart in several places. The only explanation was the poor quality of the material, because they certainly were not damaged by me. I am very disappointed with the quality of the goods, as the trousers were not like those shown in your catalogue.

I am returning the trousers in a separate package and, in the circumstances, I am asking for a complete refund. This is only fair and I will not accept a credit note.

I would like a speedy response to this letter and I look forward to hearing from you.

Yours faithfully,
Lorna Jones

Punctuation (page 28)

Checkpoint A

1

Dear Madam,

This is a letter to confirm the booking I made by telephone. As discussed, I have agreed to rent the cottage in Scotland for one week. The dates are from the 13th to the 20th of August.

I enclose a cheque for £100. This is the deposit for the booking. I realise that the balance will be due one month before the rental begins.

I would very much appreciate detailed travel directions nearer the time. I would also like to know exactly what the cottage contains. I am not quite clear how close it is to the nearest village. Any further general information you can give me would be much appreciated.

Yours faithfully,
Edward Baines

2 a I like tea, but she prefers coffee.
  b The MPs decided to vote for the measure and their constituents largely agreed with them.
  c The clients were offered an alternative holiday or they could have their money refunded.
  d The star denied she had ever said that, but the journalist insisted she had.
  e The postman delivered the letters, which came from abroad, and Linda eagerly tore the envelopes open.
3 a defines which dogs
  b defines which men
  c does not define which women
  d defines which computer program
  e gives additional information about the computer program but does not say there are others.

Activities 1 and 2

1 Job-seekers, naturally, have to prepare themselves thoroughly for the job market. Unfortunately, not everyone appreciates this fact. Of course, if someone has had professional advice, he or she is aware of the importance of making a good impression. Appearance, for example, is very important. Sadly, some applicants turn up for job interviews dressed most inappropriately.

There is, however, no mystery about choosing the appropriate clothes. Obviously, you should ask yourself what would suit the particular environment you are entering. It would not, for instance, be appropriate to turn up in a dull city suit if you were being interviewed, say, at a very trendy music shop. On the other hand, sweater and jeans would be inappropriate for an interview at a bank or insurance company.

2 a The exile returned home, which delighted his parents, who had not seen him for twenty years, because he had emigrated to Australia all those years ago.

b Since the trend seemed to be upwards, investors were drawn to invest in the Stock Market, which had been going through a bad patch lately, a development which had not surprised the experts, because world markets were so depressed.

c Although the exam had been difficult, most students felt they had done well enough to pass, because they had been so well-prepared by their teacher, whom they all admired.

Checkpoint B

16 Hudson Street,
Melchester,
MU3 7UY

Dear Sally,

How are you? It's Bank Holiday Monday and Melchester is asleep. What can I write about? Our Rover Esprit wouldn't start this morning, so we had to call in the AA. We only bought it in June.

School is boring as usual. I have Mr Jenkins for French – enough said. How's things in Bolton? Have you been watching 'The X-Files' on TV? I think it's brilliant. Mum and Dad are watching endless repeats of 'Dad's Army'. Would you believe it?

I did manage to get to Old Trafford to see England against Brazil. We were unlucky, I thought. I've made an application for the College of Applied Arts in Botham. Hope I get accepted.

Well, that's about it. Not much happening really. Drop me a line some time.

Regards,
Sarfraz

Activity 3

'The Dancing Era', the new musical by Andrew Knox that opened at the Lyric Theatre last night, should delight Mr Knox's many admirers. With a book by Tom Brice and directed by Sheila Mayhew, the show has every chance of running in London for many a month. Its hit tune will be 'Dancing mid the Tulips', but other numbers, such as 'Tripping the Fantastic' and 'Delight' should also please fans.

After its London run, the show is tipped for Sydney, New York and Paris. Stuart Mackenzie, the chief backer of the show, stated that Lena Bjorn, the star of the show, has been signed on a long-term contract. It should have earned its investment back by Easter and by Christmas it should have made millions in profit. 'This can only be good for British theatre,' said Mr Mackenzie.

Activity 4

'Let me see, let me see,' said the crazy inventor. 'You want me to make a time machine. Is that right?'

'Exactly!' said Michael. 'I want to travel into the future.'

'That's easy!' the inventor said emphatically.

'If it is so easy,' said Michael, 'why haven't you done it before now?'

'No one has ever asked me to. Anyway, I've been too busy with the present to bother with the future.'

'But you will do it?' asked Michael.

'Of course,' said the inventor. 'I said I would and I will.'

'When will you start? You see, I have to get into the future as soon as possible.'

'You want it yesterday, then,' joked the inventor. 'Don't be in such a hurry.'

'I have a special reason for haste,' said Michael, 'but I can't tell you about it.'

'Your reasons don't concern me,' replied the inventor, 'but the challenge does.'

'Let's get on with it, then,' said Michael. 'Time is getting on.'

Activity 5

1 a I think this is the loveliest line that Shakespeare wrote: 'Shall I compare thee to a summer's day?'

b These are the teams left in the draw for the next round of the cup: Blackburn, Chelsea, Bristol Rovers, Everton, Sunderland, Leeds and Tranmere Rovers.

c For the best actor award, the following have been nominated: Robert de Niro, Tom Cruise, Tom Hanks, Jim Carrey and Gary Oldman.

d The Brontë sisters wrote some of the best novels in the English language: 'Wuthering Heights', 'Jane Eyre' and 'Villette'.

2 Producing a competent curriculum vitae is essential for all job-seekers. A CV should not only give essential information; it should also represent the applicant in a favourable light. Among the features of an impressive CV are the following: neatness of presentation and logical organisation of material; accuracy of spelling, punctuation and grammar; a detailed account of the applicant's previous history; a clear and concise list of previous work experience; an accurate account of relevant educational qualifications; the willingness to give an impression of the applicant's personality and interests.

Activity 6

It's not really that surprising that the United Nations has lost much of its authority. Its authority only comes from the efforts that the various member nations make to add to the organisation's credibility.

Sadly, the interests of the individual countries usually come before those of the UN. It's a fact that some members preach co-operation among the nations of the world, but practise power politics. The UN depends on the goodwill of its members; its reputation is only as high as that of its member states.

Wars cannot be prevented by the United Nations. Its primary functions are to reconcile enemies and to provide means of helping impoverished areas of the world. It's a great pity that the basic beliefs of its charter seem to have been forgotten by its most prominent supporters.

Writing in paragraphs
(page 43)

Checkpoint A

Hampton councillors will be asked at the next council meeting to approve the construction of a new leisure centre in Eastern Road. This is one of the options Hampton's Sports and Entertainment Officer, John Jones, will recommend to the Leisure Committee. The construction will result in the closing of the temporary car park.

The majority of the residents in the Eastern Road area who responded to the recent questionnaire circulated to householders by the council supported the changes. Residents claimed the leisure centre would improve the image of the area. The resulting traffic increase was of much less consequence.

Indeed, a sizeable proportion of residents recommended that residents' parking should be introduced and the leisure centre should have an underground car park. However, the Sports and Entertainment Officer says this would not be feasible. His recommendations about parking facilities is a suitable compromise, he claims.

Activity 1

(Sample answers)

a Drug addiction is a growing problem among young people in many countries nowadays. Surveys show an increasing number of teenage addicts. Addiction is often linked to poverty and unemployment. In their despair, youngsters are turning to the easy relief of drugs without realising the damage they are doing to their bodies. The Government must do something to combat this problem.

b The introduction of a national lottery has been a major success. However, lotteries also have their critics. These people say lotteries encourage greed and they recommend that the prizes be spread as widely as possible. Nevertheless, millions of people buy lottery tickets, allowing many charities to benefit from the money raised.

c Job satisfaction is equally as important as salary in choosing a career. If you do not like what you spend your working life doing, then no salary can compensate for that. Many young people make that mistake. They choose a job because it offers higher wages and then find they cannot stand it. You have to like the way you earn your living.

d Equal opportunities for men and women must be a feature of the workplace. Unfortunately, that is not always the case. Many firms still do not see the need to encourage women to apply for senior management positions. That is why comparatively few women are represented at board level, for example. A radical change of attitude is required among business firms.

Activity 2

(Sample answers)

2 Performing well at a job interview is dependent on numerous factors. Firstly, you must make sure you arrive in plenty of time for the appointment. You do not want to appear flustered and out-of-breath because you have had to rush to get there.

Secondly, making the right impression through your appearance is a plus. No one will be impressed if someone turns up for an important interview badly dressed or looking scruffy. Give some thought to what you will wear and what would be appropriate.

During the interview, try to make direct eye contact with the particular person who is asking you questions. There is nothing worse than looking at an interviewee who is gazing at the floor or around the room. Good eye contact is a sign that you are honest and sincere.

Clarity of speech and thought before answering is also an obvious advantage. Most people are nervous during interviews. It is best to acknowledge that and then conquer it. With the best will in the world, interviewers cannot give credit to applicants who mumble or freeze.

Lastly, try to avoid appearing dogmatic in your views. You must make the interviewing panel think you will be able to co-operate with your colleagues. You must have some views of your own. No one wants to employ an individual without real personality. It is a tricky balance to get right.

Spelling (page 50)

Activities 1 and 2

1 It was during the reign of George II that the Jacobites made their last serious attempt to seize the throne. Charles Edward Stuart, known as the Young Pretender, landed on the west coast of Scotland in 1745, and was welcomed by the chiefs of powerful clans. Bonnie Prince Charlie, usually portrayed as a glamorous figure in fiction and films, was, in fact, a weak and vacillating man, who found it difficult to communicate with his generals because of his inadequate English. However, the rebellion started promisingly when the Jacobite armies were granted entry into Edinburgh without a fight.

2

Dear Sir

Nowadays we're (we are) subjected, more and more, to noise levels that would have been quite unacceptable a few years ago. I am certain that any political party that made a pledge to impose bans on unnecessary noise in public places would gain in popularity. There seems to be no ceiling on the level of noise that is acceptable in our society. Walkmans, motor bikes, road drills and car horns are only a few of the irritations that can plague our streets. Frequently, one reads about neighbours coming to blows or going to court because of the noise inflicted on one party by another. Where will it all end? Let's face it: we're (we are) a nation of noisy louts. Courtesy seems to have gone from our way of life.

Yours faithfully
Alfred Grudge

PART B

Communications: letters, memos, notes, faxes and e-mails

(page 61)

Checkpoint A
a semi-formal
b very formal
c very informal
d formal

Activity 1
(Sample letters)
a

Dear Dorothy,
    I got your letter saying you'd be at my party on the 8th of March at 7.30. That's great and I'm really looking forward to seeing you there. So are my parents. Just bring yourself, that'll be enough.
                    Love,
                    Sylvia

b

Dear Mr Wilson,
    You may remember that I worked in your firm's stores during the school holidays last summer. I am writing because I have just left school and am interested in gaining permanent employment with you. I would consider any position that you have available.
    I am really keen to work for your firm, as I enjoyed working there last summer. I hope that you will be able to offer me something. I am available for interview at any time. I look forward to hearing from you.

                    Yours sincerely,
                    Rodney Hyde

c

Dear Madam,
    Thank you for your recent order. Unfortunately, we are experiencing difficulties with our suppliers, so there will be some delay in forwarding the goods to you. Be assured that we are doing everything we can to meet your order and that as soon as we receive the goods from the suppliers, we will send them to you.
    Once again, please accept our sincere apologies for the delay.
    We will be communicating with you in the very near future.

                    Yours faithfully,

                    Laura Mason
                    Dispatch Manager

Activity 2

a

> Dear Ms Ho
>
> I have pleasure in enclosing a cheque for £325.00. This represents the amount due to you for the work you did for us during the week beginning 26 May.
>
> I would like to raise the possibility of your doing further work for us in the month of July. At present, we are not sure of the dates during which we would require your services, but I would like to check your availability in general terms now. I would appreciate your letting me know whether you could fit in some work for us around this time.
>
> Please let me know as soon as you can. I look forward to hearing from you.
>
> Yours sincerely
>
> Jill Paxton
> Company Secretary

b

> Dear Mr Hampton,
> I am writing to protest about the treatment of veal calves at our local port, which is in the constituency you represent.
> I want to make it clear that I am not a rabid animal rights protester, but merely a concerned citizen who is appalled at the cruel treatment these defenceless animals receive. To transport these animals by sea to the continent where they endure a long period of imprisonment confined in small crates is not acceptable. I hope you are making representations to the firms who profit from this trade. I have read some of your speeches about animal rights and I am sure that you are as concerned as I am about this continuing cruelty.
> I felt I wanted to voice my concern directly to you, so that you know that some of your constituents are very worried by this issue. I would appreciate a response to my letter.
>   Yours sincerely,
>   Valerie Long

Checkpoint B

a very informal; from friend to friend suggesting social occasion.

b formal; from 'boss' to employees, reminding them of deadline and regulations.

c quite formal; from someone like a department head to an assistant, possibly a secretary, asking him to carry out a task and reminding him where she will be and how she can be contacted.

Note taking, summarising, report writing (page 80)

Checkpoint A

a

> Dear Mr Smith
> The books that you ordered should be delivered by the 30th of this month. Unfortunately, there has been a problem at our usual printers and the reprinting of some titles has been delayed.
> However, I should also inform you that we normally ask customers to send in orders at least a month before delivery is required.
> I also enclose a list of deleted titles that will no longer be available. If you have any queries, please contact our sales department on 01453 764328, ext 21.
> Yours sincerely
> Geoff Langton, Sales Manager

b

Dear Ms Clough

I am sorry that you were dissatisfied with your recent stay at The Imperial, Linden. We consider the Imperial to be the flagship hotel of our group and we are concerned that you had so many complaints about standards and service.

I have personally contacted the Imperial manager to discuss the details of your complaints. On his behalf, I apologise for the inadequacies of the dinner. He did stress, however, that it is preferable to raise these matters at the time. As far as the other complaints are concerned, we are, at present, refurbishing the hotel and standards are accordingly not as high as we would like them to be.

In the circumstances, we would like to offer you, as compensation, two nights free accommodation with dinner included at the Imperial or any other hotel in the group. This offer is open until the end of May next year.

I hope you find this satisfactory and that we can look forward to your being our guest again in the near future.

Yours sincerely

Claire Michie

Group Manager

Activity 1

(Sample summary)

During lengthy discussion about working as a team, some employees welcomed the idea and suggested an external adviser.

Others stressed the need for better knowledge of what people were doing and thinking.

Opponents of the idea said that teamwork was good enough at present. Some opposed an external adviser, others said a team-building course could be run by an internal staff member. Worry was also expressed about the cost.

Teamwork was generally seen as central to business success. Not enough information was communicated from top to bottom and a 'them' and 'us' attitude was too prevalent. This issue will be raised at the next meeting.

ANSWERS

PART C
PRACTICE TESTS

INTRODUCTION

The three practice tests on pages 120–39 are modelled on the following English test papers that are taken by pupils at the end of Key Stage 3: English Paper 1 (Levels 4–7) reading and writing, and Extension Paper (Level 8 and exceptional performance).

The information below tells you how the tests work and it applies to all three tests. You will get best value out of the tests if you treat them as 'real' tests – that is
• follow the guidelines below   • time yourself.

Paper 1
At the beginning of the tests, you have 15 minutes to read the paper and make notes, but during this preparation time you are not allowed to start writing your answers.

You then have 1 hour 30 minutes to write your answers.

You must answer all of the questions in Section A and Section B.

You then choose one question to answer from Section C.

The guidelines for the tests indicate the following times that you should spend on each part of the paper, to help you to avoid running out of time on the test as a whole.

Question 1	about 10 minutes	Question 2	about 20 minutes
Question 3	about 20 minutes	Question 4	about 40 minutes

Warning: these timings fill the whole 1 hour 30 minutes, so it is crucial to realise that they include the time you need for checking. It is important to allow time for **checking**, especially in Section C where you will be assessed on the **accuracy** of your grammar, spelling and punctuation, as well as on how well you organise and express your ideas. It is all too easy to be inaccurate when you are working on a timed test, so *leave time to check so that you don't waste marks*.

Extension paper
You have 1 hour 30 minutes to complete the test.
You must answer both questions 1 and 2.

Warning: It is important to allow at least 10 minutes at the end for **checking**, especially in question 2 where you will be assessed on the **accuracy** of your grammar, spelling and punctuation, as well as how well you express your ideas. *Remember to leave time to check so that you don't waste marks*.

PRACTICE TEST 1

PAPER 1

Section A
Read the following passage. Then answer question 1 and question 2.

The writer is looking back on his childhood spent in the north of England.

When we had the shop, Christmas was a complicated and busy time. Almost everyone wanted to collect their turkeys at the last minute – or have them delivered. As a teenager, I would help with the deliveries. I could manage a couple on my bike at a time (two were always easier to balance than one) but though Dad suggested it often, I refused to fix a wire basket in front. As long   5
as I got the job done somehow, why should I ruin the appearance of my bike, which, next only to my radio, was my most valued possession?

The huge wooden refrigerator – more a wardrobe than a fridge, covering an entire wall of the cellar – was packed full of pink carcasses in December. It clicked shut with a grand mechanical cadence. And when the fierce motor   10
down on the left-hand side, complete with fly-wheel and metal guard, kicked on, a huge chugging noise juddered into the living room above.

On my sixth birthday, while I was playing a game of hide-and-seek with friends, I decided that the fridge would make a brilliant hiding place. I put on a couple of sweaters, crawled in and, with a bit of effort, managed to pull the   15
door shut. Just a few seconds in that cramped, dark, freezing place, however, and I was ready to quit. What I had not realised was that once the door had clicked, I wouldn't be able to open it from the inside.

My thumping and yelling were almost drowned out by the growl of the motor and the shouts of the game. Still, it could not have been more than a   20
couple of minutes before someone in the room above heard me and came to my rescue. When I was brought out I was in a state of suffocated terror, screaming still but almost incapable of speech. For months afterwards I had nightmares about the incident and would wake up in a sweat, inarticulate with claustrophobia and panic.   25

The fridge also figured in my first major rebellion over food. When I was ten or thereabouts, Dad and I drove down in a van to collect a number of birds from a turkey farm. Some turkeys were having their heads chopped off, some their feathers plucked, some were still running around gobbling. I was so unhappy at the thought of the very birds I was looking at turning into the   30
lifeless mounds that stocked our fridge that I promised I wouldn't eat my Christmas turkey, then or ever. Despite the aroma of the stuffing to tempt me and my father's scoffing to goad me, I kept my resolve for one Christmas.

from *An Equal Music* by Vikram Seth

Answer question 1 and question 2. **Remember** to spend less time on question 1 than the other questions.

Refer to words and phrases in the passage to support your ideas.

1. **What is described in this passage that might give you the impression that the writer in his childhood was independent and determined?**

   In your answer you should comment on:
   - his work as a delivery boy;
   - his attitude to eating meat.

   6 marks

2. **How does the writer communicate how frightening his experience of being shut in the refrigerator was?**

   In your answer you should comment on:
   - the way the fridge is described;
   - the way he reacts when he realises the fridge is locked;
   - his later reaction to the experience.

   11 marks

Section B
Read the passage below.

The writer is stating that the way we say something is just as important as what we say.

When we open our mouths to say something, we usually feel we are just talking, but what we say and how we say it are chosen from a great range of possibilities. And others react to our choices, just as they react to the clothes we wear, which serve the practical purpose of covering us up and keeping us warm, but also give impressions about the kind of people we are, and our attitudes toward the occasion. Wearing a three-piece suit may signal a formal (or stuffy) style or respect for the occasion; wearing jeans may signal a casual (or scruffy) style or not taking the occasion seriously. Personalities like formal and casual, stuffy and scruffy, and attitudes like respect or lack of it are also signalled by ways of talking. 10

Everything that is said must be said in some way – in some tone of voice, at some rate of speed, with some intonation and loudness. We may or may not consciously consider *what* to say before speaking. Rarely do we consciously consider *how* to say it, unless the situation is obviously loaded: for example, a job interview, a public address, firing someone, or breaking off a personal 15 relationship. And we almost never make deliberate decisions about whether to raise or lower our voice and pitch, whether to speed up or slow down. But these are signals by which we interpret each other's meaning and decide what we think of each other's comments – and each other.

Conversational style isn't something extra, added on like a frosting on a cake. 20 It's the very stuff of which the communication cake is made.

from *That's Not What I Meant!* by Deborah Tannen

Now answer question 3. Refer to words and phrases in the passage to support your ideas.

3. How does the passage try to persuade you that the style in which we talk to people is extremely important?

In your answer you should comment on:

- the comparisons the writer uses to illustrate what she means about how we say things;
- what she has to say about the tone of voice we use;
- how we interpret what others say to us;
- what she means by 'the very stuff of which the communication cake is made' (line 21).

11 marks

Section C

This section of the paper is a test of writing. You will be assessed on:

- *your ideas and the way you organise and express them;*
- *your ability to write clearly, using paragraphs and accurate grammar, spelling and punctuation.*

*Choose **ONE** of the following:*

4. EITHER

a) **Write a letter to your local newspaper commenting on something in your local area that is a source of possible danger to young people (e.g. a very busy traffic junction, a run-down disused factory).**

In your letter make suggestions about what you would like to see being done to remove the danger. Begin your letter *Dear Editor* and end it with your signature.

OR

b) **Write about a frightening experience that could have resulted in injury.**

- You can write about a real or imaginary event;
- try to build up a feeling of danger and tension.

OR

c) The passage above tries to tell us about how important the tone in which we speak to one another is.

Imagine you have been given a chance to talk to your class about a subject you think is important.

Write your speech trying to persuade your classmates to support your views.

33 marks

EXTENSION PAPER

Read the following two passages. They describe two different places.

Then answer the two questions which follow. You will be asked to write about **both** *of the passages.*

Passage A

This passage is from 'America Day by Day', a travel book by the writer Simone de Beauvoir. It is a description of a trip to the top of the Empire State Building in New York.

The Empire State Building

I go to the top of the Empire State Building. You buy tickets on the ground floor in an office that seems like a tourist bureau. One dollar. Twice the price of a movie ticket. There are a lot of visitors, probably people from St Louis or Cincinnati. We are directed towards the express elevators that go in a single bound to the eightieth floor. There, you have to change to reach the   5
top – a real vertical journey. Passing through a lobby where they sell miniature Empire State Buildings and different sorts of souvenirs, you reach a large glassed-in hall. There's a bar with tables and armchairs. People press their noses against the glass. In spite of the violent wind, I go out and walk around this gallery where spectacular suicides occur several times a year. I see   10
Manhattan narrowing to the south toward the point of its peninsula (or, rather, island) and spreading northward; I see Brooklyn, Queens, Staten Island, the ocean with its islands, the continental edge lapped by the sea and penetrated by two sluggish rivers. The geographic plan is so clear; the water's luminous presence reveals the original earthly element with such clarity that   15
the houses are forgotten, and I see New York as a piece of the virgin planet. The rivers, archipelago, curves, and peninsula belong to prehistory; the sea is ageless. By contrast, the simplicity of the perpendicular streets makes them look extremely young. This city has only just been born; it covers a light crust of rocks older than the Flood. Yet when the lights come on from the Bronx to   20
the Battery, from New Jersey to Brooklyn, the sea and the sky are merely the setting: the city confirms the rule of man, which is the truth of the world.

from America Day by Day by Simone de Beauvoir

Passage B

This passage is from 'A Better Class of Person' by the writer John Osborne. It is a description of the area to the south east of London to which his family moved when he was a boy in the 1930s.

Stoneleigh

By 1936, my father's health had recovered enough for him to go back to his work as an advertising copywriter. Some kind of reconciliation must have been effected between my parents as they now set about living together under the same roof. We moved out of London, away from Fulham, the beginning of a change in things for all of us.   5

In the mid-1930s the Waterloo to Effingham Junction line fingered its way as so many others did into the Surrey countryside. Although it was still possible to keep sheep and cows in the East End during the Second World War it seemed to me that the railway led into an open, light and muted world without trams, with few buses – and these green instead of red. During the next ten   10
years I grew to know almost every house and building and factory, the signs on them, the sheds in the back gardens, on the thirty-minute ride to our new house. Clapham Junction, home of Arding and Hobbs; Wimbledon with its stuffed St Bernard railway dog in his glass case on the platform (the grave gaze of this heroic animal made the change worthwhile); next, Raynes Park, with   15
Carter's Seed factory on the left, where my mother was later to work for a pittance during the early days of the war; Motspur Park, small factories and houses gathered round a pub, the Earl Beatty; then, Worcester Park, the village Neasden of its time. And Stoneleigh, where we came to live. The developers' fingers hesitated briefly before ploughing onwards, and paused to spread   20
haphazard speculative tentacles. Beyond Stoneleigh were Ewell West and Epsom, a rather unappealing Victorian town being changed into a new, bright, brick-and-cement dormitory like others that became Reigate, Redhill, Leatherhead and Dorking. But beyond them lay the Downs; Effingham Junction nudged countryside which still had a few secrets left.   25

Stoneleigh itself was a station surrounded by groups of housing estates. Coming off the concrete railway bridge on either side were 'Shopping Parades'. In the middle was Stoneleigh Hotel, which was not an hotel at all but a by-pass Tudor pub where my mother was to work throughout the war and for several years after. The Parades consisted of a small Woolworth's, the   30
dry cleaner's, newsagents and a twopenny library, butchers, florists and empty shops which had not yet been sold, gaps in the townscape, corners which had not yet been built on, patches of fields and stubble between houses and shops. It was not Stockbroker's Tudor but Bankclerk's Tudor. The ribbons of streets were empty most of the day except for occasional women   35
on their way to the Parades, pushing prams along the clean pavements with their grass verges, fresh as last week's graves.

from A Better Class of Person by John Osborne

Answer question 1 and question 2.

1. Compare the ways the writers describe the two different places.

You should consider:

- the writers' choice of detail and language;
- the feelings and attitudes of the writers to the places they are describing;
- which passage impresses you more, and why.

18 marks

2. *Concentrate on the quality of your writing. You will be assessed on your use of spelling, grammar and punctuation, and the way you express and organise your ideas.*

Choose one of the following topics. Write about 200 to 300 words.

EITHER

a) **Write about your experience of visiting a city or foreign country you had never been to before.**

Concentrate on communicating what was exciting and different about this new place.

OR

b) **Write about what you like about towns and what you like about the countryside.**

Comment on what you think are some of the advantages and disadvantages of living in a city and/or in the countryside.

18 marks

PRACTICE TEST 2

PAPER 1

Section A

Read the following passage.

Then answer question 1 and question 2.

This story is set in India. Ammu with her two children, Estha and Rahel, who are twins, accompanied by their grand-aunt Baby Kochamma, have gone to the cinema to see the film, 'The Sound of Music'.

The Torch Man shone his light on the pink tickets. Row J. Numbers 17, 18, 19, 20. Estha, Ammu, Rahel, Baby Kochamma. They squeezed past irritated people who moved their legs this way and that to make space. The seats of their chairs had to be pulled down. Baby Kochamma held Rahel's seat down while she climbed on. She wasn't heavy enough, so the chair $\qquad$ 5 folded her into herself like sandwich stuffing, and she watched from between her knees. Two knees and a fountain. Estha, with more dignity than that, sat on the edge of his chair.

The shadows of the fans were on the sides of the screen where the picture wasn't.

Off with the torch. On with the World Hit. $\qquad$ 10

The camera soared up into the skyblue (car-coloured) Austrian sky with the clear, sad sound of church bells.

Far below, on the ground, in the courtyard of the abbey, the cobblestones were shining. Nuns walked across it. Like slow cigars. Quiet nuns clustered quietly around their Reverend Mother, who never read their letters. They $\qquad$ 15 gathered like ants round a crumb of toast. Cigars around a Queen Cigar. No hair on their knees. No melons in their blouses. And their breath like peppermint. They had complaints to make to their Reverend Mother. Sweetsinging complaints. About Julie Andrews, who was still up in the hills, singing *The Hills Are Alive with the Sound of Music* and was, once $\qquad$ 20 again, late for mass.

> *She climbs a tree and scrapes her knee*

the nuns squeaked musically.

> *Her dress has got a tear.*
> *She waltzes on her way to Mass* $\qquad$ 25
> *And whistles on the stair . . .*

People in the audience were turning around.

'Shhh!' they said.
Shh! Shh! Shh! $\qquad$ 30

And underneath her wimple
she has curlers in her hair!

There was a voice from outside the picture. It was clear and true, cutting through the fan-whirring, peanut-crunching darkness. There was a nun in the audience. Heads twisted round like bottle caps. Black-haired backs of heads became faces with mouths and moustaches. Hissing mouths with teeth like sharks. Many of them. Like stickers on a card. 35

'Shhh!' they said together.

It was Estha who was singing. A nun with a puff. An Elvis Pelvis Nun. He couldn't help it. 40

'Get him out of here!' the Audience said, when they found him.

Shutup or Getout. Getout or Shutup.

The Audience was a Big Man. Estha was a Little Man, with the tickets.

'Estha, for heaven's sake, shut UP!' Ammu's fierce whisper said.

So Estha shut UP. The mouths and moustaches turned away. But then, without warning, the song came back, and Estha couldn't stop it. 45

'Ammu, can I go and sing it outside?' Estha said (before Ammu smacked him). 'I'll come back after the song.'

'But don't ever expect me to bring you out again,' Ammu said. 'You're embarrassing *all* of us.' 50

But Estha couldn't help it. He got up to go. Past angry Ammu. Past Rahel concentrating through her knees. Past Baby Kochamma. Past the Audience that had to move its legs again. Thiswayandthat. The red sign over the door said EXIT in a red light. Estha EXITED.

In the lobby, the orangedrinks were waiting. The lemondrinks were waiting. 55 The melty chocolates were waiting. The electric blue foamleather car-sofas were waiting. The *Coming Soon!* posters were waiting.

Estha Alone sat on the electric blue foamleather car-sofa, in the Abhilash Talkies Princess Circle lobby, and sang. In a nun's voice, as clear as clean water. 60

But how do you make her stay
And listen to all you say?

from *The God of Small Things* by Arundhati Roy

Answer question 1 and question 2 (overleaf). **Remember** to spend less time on question 1 than the other questions.

Refer to words and phrases in the passage to support your ideas.

1. **What impression do you get about Estha's reaction to the film?**

   In your answer you should comment on:
   - how he behaves in the cinema;
   - what he does when he leaves.

   6 marks

2. **What does the writer tell us about the reaction of the cinema audience to Estha's singing?**

   In your answer you should comment on:
   - their first reaction to Estha's singing;
   - what they shout out;
   - how much the audience was interested in the movie;
   - how the writer describes the audience, including her unusual use of capital letters.

   11 marks

Section B

Read this newspaper article about young people doing part-time jobs.

Two million Brits aged 10 to 16 work part-time – two out of five children aged 10 or over and two out of three over-15s hold part-time jobs. Yet an estimated two-thirds of children who work are doing so illegally and many others are ripped off by miserly employers who give less than the average rates of pay for jobs typically done by youngsters, according to new research from Abbey National. [10]

The average weekly pay for 10 to 16-year-olds is £14.03. Girls earn an average £2.75 per hour and boys £1.93, largely because girls are more likely to do shop work which tends to be more highly paid, though in general girls are less likely to work than boys. [15]

One in three schoolchildren who work have more than one job. Half of all children who work have delivery jobs while almost one in five works in a shop. Part-time jobs as cinema ushers, paying an average £5 per hour, and as supermarket checkout operators at £4.50 an hour, tend to be the best-paid positions to go for. Among the worst- [20] [25]

paid are paperboys or girls who earn £7 a week, and chip shop assistants, who make just £1.20 an hour, according to Abbey National. [30]

Of the high proportion of children working illegally, a quarter are under the minimum age, almost one in five starts work before 7am on a weekday and one in five works after 7pm in the evening, says Abbey National, which has published a free guide to make parents aware of their children's rights at work and how to protect them. [35]

Though children are obviously being exploited in such situations, parents can at least rest assured that it is the employer, not the child, who is breaking the law. [40]

The minimum age to start paid work is 14, though in some areas local authority by-laws allow 13-year-olds to do certain jobs such as delivering newspapers, serving in shops, working in hairdressing salons, offices, cafés and riding stables. [45] [50]

from *The Guardian*, 14 October 2000

Now answer question 3. Refer to words and phrases in the article to support your ideas.

3. How does the article aim to persuade you that children are not being treated fairly when they take on part-time jobs?

In your answer you should comment on:

- how the writer has used particular words and phrases to persuade you children are getting a raw deal;
- the examples given of average pay and hours of work;
- whether the writer has made a strong argument that children are exploited.

11 marks

Section C

This section of the paper is a test of writing. You will be assessed on:

- *your ideas and the way you organise and express them;*
- *your ability to write clearly, using paragraphs and accurate grammar, spelling and punctuation.*

Choose ONE of the following:

4. EITHER

a) Imagine you are a local employer. (You can decide the line of business you are in, e.g. a local supermarket or a hairdressing salon.)

   Write a leaflet that will be distributed to local schools to attract young people to work for your business.

   In your leaflet you should describe:

   - the part-time jobs that are available to young people;
   - the pay and hours of work;
   - the advantages of taking such a part-time job.

OR

b) **Write about a very special visit to a cinema or theatre.**

   You could:

   - write about a real or imaginary event;
   - try to communicate what was so memorable about the occasion.

OR

c) The article tries to persuade the reader that many children are being exploited when they take part-time jobs.

   Imagine you have been given an opportunity to talk in a year or house assembly. Choose an issue you feel strongly about.

   Write your speech trying to persuade your listeners to support your views.

33 marks

EXTENSION PAPER

Read the following two passages. They are both about parent–child relationships.

Then answer the two questions that follow. You will be asked to write about **both** *of the passages.*

Passage A
This extract is from 'Man and Boy', a novel by Tony Parsons. It is about his experience of father–son relationships.

Father and Son

Every father is a hero to his son. At least when they are too small to know any better.

Pat thinks I can do anything right now. He thinks I can make the world bend to my will – just like Han Solo or Indiana Jones. I know that one day soon Pat will work out that there are a few differences between Harrison   5
Ford and his old dad. And when he realises that I don't actually own a bullwhip or a light sabre, he will never look at me in quite the same way again.

But before they grow out of it, all sons think their dad is a hero. It was a bit different with me and my dad. Because my dad really was a hero. He had a   10
medal to prove it and everything.

If you saw him in his garden or in his car, you would think he was just another suburban dad. Yet in a drawer in the living room of the pebble-dashed semi where I grew up there was a Distinguished Service Medal that he had won during the war. I spent my childhood pretending to be a hero. My   15
dad was the real thing.

The DSM – that's important. Only the Victoria Cross is higher, and usually you have to die before they give you that. If you saw my dad in a pub or on the street, you would think you knew all about him, just by looking at his corny jumper or his balding head or his family saloon or his choice of   20
newspaper. You would think that you knew him. And you would be dead wrong.

from *Man and Boy* by Tony Parsons

Passage B

This extract is from 'Starcarbon', a novel by Ellen Gilchrist.

Father and daughter

Jessie's baby was due on Sunday. On Thursday Daniel Hand drove out to the
Charlotte airport and got on a plane and flew to New Orleans to await the
birth. He checked into the Royal Orleans and changed shirts and got into his
rented car and drove down Saint Charles Avenue to Webster Street and found
the house where his daughter lived and got out and stood looking up at the   5
porch. He had not seen her in five months and he had no idea what to expect.
His Jessie, the jewel in his crown. His beautiful child, his skater, bike rider,
acrobat, swimmer, dancer, about to deliver a child. Well, he was a man and he
could take it. He started up the stairs to the house. She came running out to
meet him. 'Oh, Daddy,' she was screaming. 'I'm so glad you're here. I'm sooo   10
bored. It's taking forever. I can't wait to get it out. I'm going crazy waiting to
see my baby.' She hugged him fiercely to herself, and somehow the fact that
she was swollen with a baby was irrelevant. She was Jessie, making anything
she did look good.

'You need anything?' he asked. 'Is there anything I can get for you?'   15

from *Starcarbon* by Ellen Gilchrist

Answer question 1 and question 2.

1. **Compare the ways the writers describe how, in Passage A, the
   son (the 'I' of the passage) feels towards his own father and,
   in Passage B, the father feels towards his daughter, Jessie.**

   You should consider:

   - the writer's choice of detail and language;
   - the feelings expressed;
   - which piece impresses you more and why.

   18 marks

2. *Concentrate on the quality of your writing. You will be assessed on your
   use of spelling, grammar and punctuation, and the way you express and
   organise your ideas.*

   Choose one of the following topics. Write about 200 to 300 words.

   EITHER

   a) **Write about someone you admire (it could be anyone at all:
      a relative, a friend, a famous person) and communicate
      your reasons for admiring this person.**

   OR

   b) **Write a detailed description of a person (real or imaginary)
      you find interesting in some way.**

      Concentrate on using language to highlight particular characteristics
      of this person.

   18 marks

PAPER 1

Section A

Read the following story.

Then answer question 1 and question 2.

The story is set in Brighton on the south coast of England. It is about seventeen-year-old Pinky (referred to as the Boy in the passage), a small-time criminal, who suspects that some incriminating evidence, a calling card left by someone called Kolley Kibber, has been left in a restaurant. Kibber works for a newspaper that gives a prize to anyone finding one of the cards he leaves. The Boy is worried that this card will link him with the murder of Kibber.

'Was it tea you wanted, sir?' He looked sharply up with his hand under the cloth: one of those girls who creep about, he thought, as if they were afraid of their own footsteps: a pale thin girl younger than himself.

He said, 'I gave the order once.'

She apologised abjectly. 'There's been such a rush. And it's my first day. This was the only breathing spell. Have you lost something?' 5

He withdrew his hand, watching her with dangerous and unfeeling eyes. His cheek twitched again; it was the little things which tripped you up, he could think of no reason at all for having his hand under the tablecloth. She went on helpfully, 'I'll have to change the cloth again for tea, so if you've lost —' 10

In no time she had cleared the table of pepper and salt and mustard, the cutlery and the O.K. sauce, the yellow flowers, had nipped together the corners of the cloth and lifted it in one movement from the table, crumbs and all.

'There's nothing there, sir,' she said. He looked at the bare table-top and said, 'I hadn't lost anything.' She began to lay a fresh cloth for tea. She seemed to find something agreeable about him which made her talk, something in common perhaps – youth and shabbiness and a kind of ignorance in the dapper café. Already she had apparently forgotten his exploring hand. But would she remember, he wondered, if later people asked her questions? He despised her quiet, her pallor, her desire to please: did she also observe, remember . . .? 'You wouldn't guess,' she said, 'what I found here only ten minutes ago. When I changed the cloth.' 15

'Do you always change the cloth?' the Boy asked. 20

'Oh, no,' she said, putting out the tea things, 'but a customer upset his drink and when I changed it, there was one of Kolley Kibber's cards worth ten shillings. It was quite a shock,' she said, lingering gratefully with the tray, 25 'and the others don't like it. You see it's only my second day here. They say I was a fool not to challenge him and get the prize.'

'Why didn't you challenge him?'

'Because I never thought. He wasn't a bit like the photograph.'   30

'Maybe the card had been there all morning.'

'Oh, no,' she said, 'it couldn't have been. He was the first man at this table.'

'Well,' the Boy said, 'it don't make any odds. You've *got* the card.'

'Oh yes, I've got it. Only it don't seem quite fair – you see what I mean – him being so different. I *might* have got the prize. I can tell you I ran to the door   35
when I saw the card: I didn't wait.'

'And did you see him?'

She shook her head.

'I suppose,' the Boy said, 'you hadn't looked at him close. Else you'd have known.'   40

'I always look at you close,' the girl said, 'the customer, I mean. You see, I'm new. I get a bit scared. I don't want to do anything to offend. Oh,' she said aghast, 'like standing here talking when you want a cup of tea.'

'That's all right,' the Boy said. He smiled at her stiffly; he couldn't use those muscles with any naturalness. 'You're the kind of girl I like—' The words were   45
the wrong ones; he saw it at once and altered them. 'I mean,' he said, 'I like a girl who's friendly. Some of these here – they freeze you.'

'They freeze me.'

'You're sensitive, that's what it is,' the Boy said, 'like me.' He said abruptly, 'I suppose you wouldn't recognize that newspaper man again? I mean, he may   50
still be about.'

'Oh, yes,' she said, 'I'd know him. I've got a memory for faces.'

The Boy's cheek twitched. He said, 'I see you and I've got a bit in common. We ought to get together one evening. What's your name?'

'Rose.'   55

He put a coin on the table and got up. 'But your tea,' she said.

'Here we been talking, and I had an appointment at two sharp.'

'Oh, I'm sorry,' Rose said. 'You should've stopped me.'

'That's all right,' the Boy said. 'I liked it. It's only ten-past anyway – by your clock. When do you get off of an evening?'   60

'We don't close till half-past ten except on Sundays.'

'I'll be seeing you,' the Boy said. 'You an' me have things in common.'

from *Brighton Rock* by Graham Greene

*Answer question 1 and question 2. **Remember** to spend less time on question 1 than the other questions.*

Refer to words and phrases in the passage to support your ideas.

1. **What impression do you get of the kind of person Rose is?**

   In your answer you should comment on:

   • the way Rose behaves and speaks;
   • the reaction of the Boy to her;
   • the use of words and detail by the writer.

   6 marks

2. **How does the writer make you aware that the Boy is trying to win the confidence and liking of Rose?**

   In your answer you should comment on:

   • the questions he asks her;
   • the way he flatters her;
   • the tone in which he speaks;
   • what he says and does at the end of the passage.

   11 marks

Section B
Read the passage below.

It is about Yellowstone National Park in the United States, an area of great natural beauty. It discusses the necessity of finding a balance between making areas such as these accessible to the public and the need to conserve wilderness areas in their original state.

The somewhat conflicting purposes contained in the act establishing Yellowstone National Park – to 'protect and preserve' the area and to keep it a place 'for the benefit and enjoyment of the people' – have always required a certain amount of compromise.

An area cannot be preserved in its natural state if it is intruded upon by roads,   5 hotels, service stations, campgrounds, and sewage plants. Nor can most people enjoy a park as large as Yellowstone if they are allowed to enter only on foot and stay only until nightfall. Obviously some compromise is necessary – some alteration of the natural world must take place in order to accommodate the people by whom and for whom the park was established. The question, then, is   10 – and always has been – *how much* modification of the natural features is justifiable in the interest of human accessibility and convenience. The answer is complicated by the additional requirement of the National Park Service Act 1916 to 'leave it unimpaired for the enjoyment of future generations.'

Over a hundred years ago Mammoth Hot Springs was the only one of the   15 park's principal features that could easily be reached. Old Faithful and Yellowstone Canyon were each two additional days' travel by horse; Yellowstone Lake was yet another day beyond either of them. Park visitation was limited, but it could be seen that a system of roads and overnight accommodations would be needed – even at the expense of some modification of the natural state. The Grand Loop road and its related facilities were planned almost immediately after the park's establishment and were constructed as soon as funds were available. But American society has changed in those hundred years. Roads that were designed for horses and stagecoaches have been widened and regraded for use by automobiles. Facilities that were designed to accommodate only 10,000 visitors a year have been expanded to serve many times that number. Now, about 3 million people a year in a million motor vehicles use those facilities and roads – and the people and the park are again feeling the pressure.

For many years it has been generally felt that fishing is an appropriate recreational activity in a national park. To make the already good fishing here even better, several exotic species were introduced into the park's waterways. Their effects on the ecosystem were not good, however, and today the Yellowstone fisheries are more carefully managed. It may even be true, as sometimes suggested, that in a national park – where the hunting of game animals, the picking of flowers, and the collecting of rocks are considered incompatible with preservation – the catching of fish may also be inappropriate.

Yellowstone's herds of game animals were protected from hunting as early as 1883, but annual 'cropping' was practiced until the late 1960s, and predatory animals were 'controlled' by official killing as late as the 1930s. Today it is believed that human control of predators is not only unnatural, it is also unnecessary.

from *Yellowstone* by Hugh Crandall

Now answer question 3 below. Refer to words and phrases in the passage to support your ideas.

3. How does the passage try to suggest that there should be a compromise between the needs of visitors to the park and the need to preserve it in its natural state?

In your answer you should comment on:

- how the writer gives details of the requirements of visitors that affect the park;
- how the writer uses comparisons of the past with the present;
- the way the writer uses fishing, hunting and 'cropping' to illustrate some of the difficult choices that have to be made;
- the way words and phrases are used to argue a case for the preservation of the park;
- whether you think the passage helps to make clear the problems of getting the balance right between the needs of visitors and the preservation of the park.

11 marks

Section C

This section of the paper is a test of writing. You will be assessed on:

- *your ideas and the way you organise and express them;*
- *your ability to write clearly, using paragraphs and accurate grammar, spelling and punctuation.*

*Choose **ONE** of the following:*

4. EITHER

a) Imagine you are a manager of a restaurant. A customer has complained about the poor standards of service and food.

Write a letter of reply to this customer apologising for the problems and giving an explanation of why they may have occurred.

Write an address for the restaurant at the top. Begin your letter *Dear . . .* (choose any name for the customer) and end it with *Yours sincerely* and your signature.

In your letter you could write about:

- your regret that the customer has felt the need to complain;
- why the problems may have occurred;
- what you hope to do to put things right;
- how much you value the comments of customers.

OR

b) **Write about an exciting visit to an area of great natural beauty and wildness.**

You could write about:

- a real or imaginary visit to a real or imaginary area;
- try to communicate your feelings of pleasure and excitement about the visit.

OR

c) The passage about Yellowstone National Park tries to raise awareness about the need to conserve areas of great natural interest and beauty.

Imagine you have been given the opportunity to talk to your class or year about an aspect of environmental concerns that particularly interests you.

Write your speech in such a way as to persuade your listeners to support your views.

33 marks

EXTENSION PAPER

Read the following two passages. They describe childhood experiences.

Then answer the two questions that follow. You will be asked to write about **both** *of the passages.*

Passage A

This passage is from an autobiography by Storm Jameson. Whitby, the place mentioned in the passage, is a town on the coast of Yorkshire.

I can fix the month, almost to the day, when I ceased to be a child. Soon after we moved to the new house, my mother went on the last of her sea voyages. She went to Buenos Aires (pronounced by every Whitby sea-captain's family Bonnus-airs), leaving us as boarders in the private school we had been going to daily for a year. She was at sea when we went down with scarlet fever, all   5 three of us. Rather than send us to the fever hospital, it was decided to open up the house and put us in it on the top floor, in charge of a nurse and an old woman called Nightingale. We spent six or seven weeks shut up here, we were not ill, and had nothing to amuse us except a number of cardboard dress-boxes that we turned into a fleet of liners and sailed in them about the rooms.   10 On the fourth or fifth day when I woke, I glanced down at the ship moored alongside my bed, and realised in the same instant that I was an adult shut up with two children.

From this moment until we were released I endured an excruciating boredom, the worst in my life until I had to live in a house of my own – which was   15 infinitely worse. I had two books, no more – the nurse, a fool, had a theory that reading was bad for fever patients – *Kenilworth* and a copy of the *Arabian Nights* from which she had torn the opening pages as unfit for a child to read. Neither was left in my hands for longer than half an hour. Every evening I prayed avidly that God would kill her in the night. A black mamba secretes   20 less venom than a child's impotent hate.

The gap that separated me from the others widened at the speed of a galloping horse. I could no longer invent fairy-tales for them. I began to dream feverishly of *getting away* – away from Whitby, from a barren life without excitement or a chance to show that I was an exception.   25

from *Journey from the North* by Storm Jameson

This extract is from 'David Copperfield' by the nineteenth-century English novelist, Charles Dickens. David has been expelled from his school and sent by his harsh stepfather, Mr Murdstone, to work in a factory in London.

Murdstone and Grinby's trade was among a good many kinds of people, but an important branch of it was the supply of wines and spirits to certain packet ships. I forget now where they chiefly went, but I think there were some among them that made voyages both to the East and West Indies. I know that a great many empty bottles were the consequence of this traffic, 5 and that certain men and boys were employed to examine them against the light, and reject those that were flawed, and to rinse and wash them. When the empty bottles ran short, there were labels to be pasted on full ones, or corks to be fitted to them, or seals to be put upon the corks, or finished bottles to be packed in casks. All this work was my work, and of the boys 10 employed upon it I was one.

There were three or four of us, counting me. My working place was established in a corner of the warehouse, where Mr Quinion could see me, when he chose to stand up on the bottom rail of his stool in the counting-house, and look at me through a window above the desk. Hither, on the first 15 morning of my so auspiciously beginning life on my own account, the oldest of the regular boys was summoned to show me my business. His name was Mick Walker, and he wore a ragged apron and a paper cap. He informed me that his father was a bargeman, and walked, in a black velvet head-dress, in the Lord Mayor's Show. He also informed me that our principal associate 20 would be another boy whom he introduced by the – to me – extraordinary name of Mealy Potatoes. I discovered, however, that this youth had not been christened by that name, but that it had been bestowed upon him in the warehouse, on account of his complexion which was pale or mealy. Mealy's father was a waterman, who had the additional distinction of being a 25 fireman, and was engaged as such at one of the large theatres; where some relation of Mealy's – I think his little sister – did Imps in the Pantomimes.

No words can express the secret agony of my soul as I sunk into this companionship; compared these henceforth every-day associates with those of my happier childhood – not to say with Steerforth, Traddles, and the rest 30 of those boys; and felt my hopes of growing up to be a learned and distinguished man crushed in my bosom. The deep remembrance of the sense I had, of being utterly without hope now; of the shame I felt in my position; of the misery it was to my young heart to believe that day by day what I had learned, and thought, and delighted in, and raised my fancy and my 35 emulation up by, would pass away from me, little by little, never to be brought back any more, cannot be written. As often as Mick Walker went away in the course of that afternoon, I mingled my tears with the water in which I was washing the bottles; and sobbed as if there were a saw in my own breast, and it were in danger of bursting. 40

from David Copperfield by Charles Dickens

Answer question 1 and question 2.

1. **Compare the ways the writers describe the experiences and feelings of the young persons in the passages: the 'I' (the young Storm Jameson) of Passage A and David, the 'I' of Passage B.**

   You should consider:

   - the writers' choice of language and detail;
   - the feelings of the young people described by the writers;
   - which passage is more interesting to you and why.

   18 marks

2. *Concentrate on the quality of your writing. You will be assessed on your use of spelling, grammar and punctuation, and the way you express and organise your ideas.*

   Choose one of the following topics. Write about 200 to 300 words.

   EITHER

   a) **Storm Jameson describes a period in her childhood when she felt very bored and resentful. Write about any time in your life when you have experienced similar feelings.**

   OR

   b) **Write a description of a place that brings out its special qualities and characteristics.**

   This place could be beautiful, ugly or dingy, frightening or awe-inspiring, or a mixture of all these aspects. Concentrate on using language effectively to create a clear image of the place. The place can be real or imaginary.

   18 marks